Giving Your Money Away

Other Books by Danny Siegel

Tzedakah, Mitzvahs, Tikkun Olam, and Jewish Values
Angels, 1980
Gym Shoes and Irises: Personalized Tzedakah, 1981
　　　　Book Two, 1987
Munbaz II and Other Mitzvah Heroes, 1988
Family Reunion: Making Peace in the Jewish Community, 1989
Mitzvahs, 1990
After the Rain, 1993
Good People, 1995
Heroes and Miracle Workers 1997
1 + 1 = 3 and 37 Other Mitzvah Principles For a Meaningful Life 2000
Danny Siegel's Bar and Bat Mitzvah Mitzvah Book: A Practical Guide
　　　　For Changing the World Through Your Simcha, 2004
Who — Me? Yes — You!: Danny Siegel's Workbook to Help You Decide
　　　　Where, When, Why, and How You Can Do Your Best Tikkun Olam, 2006

For Children
The Humongous Pushka in the Sky, 1993
Tell Me a Mitzvah (Children's stories, Kar-Ben Copies, Inc.), 1993
Mitzvah Magic: What Kids Can Do to Change the World (Kar-Ben/Lerner), 2002

Midrash and Halachah
Where Heaven and Earth touch: An Anthology of Midrash and Halachah
　　　　Book One, 1983; *Large Print Edition*, 1985, *Book Two*, 1984,
　　　　Book Three, 1985, *Combined Books One-Three*, 1988,
　　　　Hardback edition, 1989; *Soft cover*, 1995 *(Jason Aronson publishers)*,
　　　　Source Book: Selected Hebrew and Aramaic Sources, 1985

Poetry
Soulstoned, 1969
And God Braided Eve's Hair, 1976
Between Dust and Dance (with prose), 1978
Nine Entered Paradise Alive, 1980
Unlocked Doors: The Selected Poems of Danny Siegel 1969-1983, 1983
The Lord Is A Whisper at Midnight: Psalms and Prayers, 1985
The Garden, Where Wolves and Lions Do No Harm to the Sheep and Deer, 1985
Before Our Very Eyes: Readings for a Journey Through Israel, 1986
The Meadow Beyond the Meadow (1991)
A Hearing Heart (1992)

Healing
Healing: Readings and Meditations (1999)

Humor
The Unorthodox Book of Jewish Records and Lists (co-authored with Allan Gould), 1982

Giving Your Money Away

How Much, How to, Why, When, and to Whom

Danny Siegel's
Practical Guide
to Personalized Tzedakah

by Danny Siegel

THE TOWN HOUSE PRESS
Pittsboro, North Carolina

I would like to thank the following people for their help in making this book come to fruition: Dr. Michael Stulberg, Marc and Arlene Sternfeld, Merle and Allan Gould, Louise Cohen, Aaron Lansky, Professor Jeffrey Tigay, William Begal, Brayton Campbell, Barbara Kadden, Jay Feinberg, Glenn Easton, Cantor Josh Perlman, Miriam Heller, Marc Pollick, Sharon Halper, Shulamit Gittelson, Sivan Slapak, Mark Stadler, Howard Schilit, and Rabbis Joel Soffin, Neal Gold, Steven Z. Leder, David Rosenn, Gordon Fuller, Marc Greenspan, and Mark Hyman, and Dr. Gordon, Myra, Gary, and Brian Gondos. In various ways they helped me develop and articulate many of the ideas that appear in these pages. I am grateful for their assistance.

Dr. Abraham Gittelson, Arnie Draiman, and Steve and Judy Kerbel, offered important suggestions concerning the content of various chapters. They also proofread various stages of the manuscript for typographical and grammatical errors, often a thankless task. Their contributions to this book are greatly appreciated.

Naomi Eisenberger reviewed with me the entire manuscript and — besides clarifying many content issues with me — provided hundreds of invaluable stylistic suggestions. My gratitude to Naomi for her contribution to this endeavor.

Some of the Biblical translations are taken from *Tanakh, The Holy Scriptures, The New JPS Translation According to the Traditional Hebrew Text,* © 1985, The Jewish Publication Society of America, Philadelphia. Reprinted with permission of the publisher.

Book Design by Darryl Rotman Kuperstock

Library of Congress Catalogue Card Number: 2006905620
International Standard Book Number: 0-940653-51-6

First Printing: 2006

For Ordering:
   CMS Distributors/Eisenberger
   384 Wyoming Avenue
   Millburn, NJ 07041
   Phone: 973-763-9396
   Fax: 973-275-0346
   e-mail: naomike@aol.com

for

Michael Stulberg, M.D.

משה בן שלמה ז״ל ויהודית ז״ל

Gifted Healer

רופא רפואת הנפש ורפואת הגוף בחסד עליון

Mensch

א גרויסער מענטש

Good Friend of Many Years

נפשי קשורה בנפשו

וכל המקים נפש אחת...כאלו קים עולם מלא

...Whoever saves a single life —
it is as if that person has saved an entire world.

Mishnah Sanhedrin, Chapter 4, end

The opposite of love is not hate, it's indifference. The opposite of faith is not heresy, it's indifference. And, the opposite of life is not death, it's indifference. Because of indifference one dies before one actually dies.

Elie Wiesel

פעולת צדיק לחיים...

The good things a Good Person does is the very force-of-Life.

Proverbs 10:16

צדיק נקרא חיים

A Good Person is called "Life."

Avot DeRabbi Natan 34

Happiness, fun, joy

I like happy people, and I like making people happy whenever I can. It takes very little to make some people happy.

I like fun. I like fun in all its variations: goofiness, clowning around, silliness, good, clean jokes that make people laugh from their bellies to their soul. Who doesn't like to have fun and to watch others having fun as well? There is a certain exuberance to it, a positively thrilling, bursting energy. Just picture a 10-year-old going down a waterslide shouting, "Look, Eema! Look! Look!" It warms your heart.

"Joy" is harder to get a grip on. It is somewhere "higher up there". It's easy to think of and list joyous occasions. Watching the birth of your child. Stepping off the 777's ramp onto the Holy Ground of Ben Gurion Airport. Living long enough to see a student who came to you incredibly self-centered and wild grow into a real Mensch. Sitting in synagogue and hearing an adult read Torah — someone *you* taught to read Torah who never learned as a child.

Those are surely joyous occasions. But the abstract concept "joy" — it's difficult to get a handle on it. It's up there with words and concepts like "soul", "awe", and "life". I feel a need to make it more substantive and less ethereal.

Wouldn't it be a fine thing if...?

Wouldn't it be nice if you could spend your days letting people who need it have fun?

Wouldn't it be grand if you could use every resource you have to make unhappy people happy?

Wouldn't it be wonderful if you could take all the people in the world who are living in despair and give them joy — *whatever* "joy" means?

Happiness, Fun, Joy...and Money

You can.

And, just imagine! Money — of all things — is the awesome instrument that can make it happen. *Tzedakah* money.

Getting a handle on "joy"

Perhaps that's the way to get a grip on "joy" and to bring it down to earth. You do it with — of all things — money. You handle money all the time. Even with your eyes closed, you can feel what a coin is. It feels different than a button or

CD, paper clip, or door knob. Even in the darkest of rooms, you know that those are dollar bills in your hand, and you would never confuse their "feel" with a page from a newspaper, a maple leaf, or sandpaper.

All that Mitzvah-potential is in your hands, all the possibilities in the world to bring happiness, fun, and joy to so many people. *That's* real joy. *That's* שמחה של מצוה-Simcha Shel Mitzvah, The Joy of Doing this Mitzvah of Tzedakah.

Are you looking to put a little (more) joy in your life?

Maimonides teaches something most astonishing about joy:

שאין שם שמחה גדולה ומפוארה
אלא לשמח לב עניים ויתומים ואלמנות וגרים

There is no greater or more glorious joy than to bring joy to the hearts of poor people, orphans, widows, and strangers.
Laws of the Megillah and Channukah 2:17

So, there is "joy" in human existence, and there is "great joy". And there is "the greatest and most glorious joy" a person can experience in life.

No scale of 1-10 adequately defines the joy of providing for the needs of individuals living in deprived circumstances, widows, orphans, and strangers.

The joy of Tzedakah is somewhere "up there" in the millions.

Table of Contents

Exactly How Do You Decide Where to Donate Your Tzedakah Money?

Tzedakah and the Meaning of "Self"

In Conclusion — Four Stories from "Real Life"

Preliminaries

Introduction: Holy Money

Money Makes Miracles Happen

Money can make miracles happen. Not only *can* it make miracles happen, it *does* make miracles happen — through Tzedakah. Every day, everywhere that Mitzvah money is used *wisely* for the benefit of others, big miracles, medium-sized miracles, and so-called "small" miracles are happening. (There really are no "small" miracles.) Endangered, disheartened, and troubled individuals can look to good health, opportunity, and hope because of the amazing power of Tzedakah.

I am not referring only to donations of $10,000,000 here and $50,000,000 there to change the world one way or another. When I wrote the opening paragraph, I wasn't even thinking about the mega-rich donors. I had in mind the "regular" folks who may dream of having millions of dollars to give away, but in reality only have considerably more modest budgets — like you. The fact is, the more skilled you become in using your sacred Tzedakah money, the more you will come to realize that $1.00, $5.00, $18.00, $25.00, or $100 can have a profound effect on the lives of many other people. This is the true nature of the Jewish perspective on Tikkun Olam. Human needs and human nature are such that even a little Tzedakah money, well timed and judiciously placed, has such overwhelming power that you may be at a loss to believe what you can accomplish. This is true even if you are "only" one person among billions of human beings on this earth.

The material in this guide is intended for everyone: adult and child, multi-millionaire, well-to-do, middle-income, or just scraping by.

From their earliest years, young children — who may have only a few dollars to donate — will learn that *every single dollar can make a vast difference in the lives of the appropriate recipient.* Many of them already know this because they have been taught that some of their birthday presents are to be given away. And they may already know that, if they receive gifts every night of Channukah, one night's gifts are not theirs; they will be given to other kids who may not have gotten any presents. Most of all, they will know that they don't have to wait until they are 32, 47, or 61 to change the world. It may be that, with the proper training in Tzedakah, Tikkun Olam will become as close to second-nature as possible. The "me-me-me" odds will have changed so much that, later on in life, they will have already overcome many obstacles to effective and meaningful giving. Hopefully they will have understood that when they get their first paycheck with "their real hard-earned money", the thrill will include the immediate thought, "Ah, now I have that much more money to use for Tzedakah."

As for the mega-wealthy — some of this material should remind them that *every single dollar can make a vast difference in the lives of the appropriate recipient.* They are already aware that certain Tikkun Olam can only be done with millions of dollars. No waste should be tolerated even when distributing enormous sums of Tzedakah money.

People's lives change for the better every day, every hour, by *any* and *every* prudent donation of Tzedakah money. People who were living in despair, who once felt that they had no fair chance to live a Menschlich — a decent — life, now live in good health, in safety, with dignity and hope. In turn, they have a heightened, refined sense of caring and giving to others because of Tzedakah money that gave them their hope, opportunity, and a restored feeling of Life-affirmation.

Thinking Big

I am now 61 years old. I have seen innumerable situations where Mitzvah money has this incredible power, beginning from earliest childhood. My parents, Dr. Julius and Edythe Siegel, מנוחתם שלום, both lived a life of Tzedakah. Besides their own giving, they made certain that I was surrounded by their friends, people who regularly contributed their money so that others might live a Menschlich life. As a teen-ager deeply involved in United Synagogue Youth, I had a large circle of friends who *always* responded to the needs of others.

In 1975, I began to focus more intensely on the power of Tzedakah. Before leaving for Israel for a few weeks, friends and relatives had given me $955.00 to distribute to Good People doing Tikkun Olam. I found them easily, these people whom I came to call "Mitzvah heroes". I simply asked friends, "Who is doing *real* Tikkun Olam the right way?" When I got back to the United States, I issued a report for my donors describing exactly how the money had been given away on their behalf. I thought that was the end of the story. But my friends and relatives —and then casual acquaintances and strangers — continued to send me *more* money. By 1981, the Tzedakah work had grown so much, it was necessary to establish two legal entities, Ziv Tzedakah Fund in the United States and Ziv Tzedakah Foundation in Canada. Ziv now donates in Israel, North America, and in many other places throughout the world. By the time I am writing this, more than $10,000,000 has been given to me to be given away.

Because of my personal experiences, it is easy to understand why I encourage my audiences and students to Think Big. In modern Jewish history, the accomplishments of Theodore Herzl should give you a sense of just how much the world can change because of the efforts of a single person. In early American history, the same can be said of George Washington and Thomas Jefferson, or more recently, Martin Luther King and Rosa Parks. Think of Jonas Salk, or the inventor of the CAT scan. All of these people repaired broken parts of the world and people's lives. I believe that Tzedakah has *that much* power to change the world...even more than I can ever imagine.

I firmly believe that *anyone* can use that power of Tzedakah to change the world...even more than they could possibly ever imagine.

Money and Mitzvah Money

Our consciousness is saturated with money. Any standard thesaurus lists more than 50 words related to money, from "cold cash" to "mazuma" and "smackers", "cabbage" to "moola" and "scratch". Even if we don't understand what they mean, we have heard the terms "fiduciary", "amortization", and "accrued interest". How many scathing articles have you read about garish and tasteless materialism and senseless waste? Certainly too many to recall.

You have heard the phrase, "Money is the root of all evil" since you were a child. Tzedakah money — combined with Gemillut Chassadim, acts of caring, lovingkindness — is the diametric opposite of this view. This book is about generosity and caring. (I leave *The Theory and Practice of Greed and Vulgar Consumption* to others.) In these pages I will take the well-worn phrase "Money makes the world go 'round" and simply add one word — "Tzedakah". "*Tzedakah money* makes the world go 'round". If you keep *that* phrase in mind, you will get a more accurate *Jewish* picture of exactly how money, indeed, makes the world go 'round.

Jewish Values and the Practical Guide to Giving Jewishly

The purpose of this book is two-fold: (1) to present the unique Jewish approach to using your Tzedakah money to change the world, and (2) to offer very practical techniques, procedures, real-Life examples, and reminders that will hopefully help you use your own Tzedakah money more wisely, efficiently, and *Jewishly*. Various chapters will explain why, how much (whether vast sums or a few dollars), when (and when not), and to whom Jewish people might want to give Tzedakah. Among other issues, I will explore how to find worthy recipients and appropriate Tzedakah advisors, and how modern tools such as e-mail and the internet can be used to make your giving easier, more effective, and more meaningful.

The material relating to the Jewish way of giving is not difficult to understand, and the techniques are relatively few in number and easy to manage. In fact, while there *are* some complex issues involved in giving Tzedakah, one of the main purposes of this guide is to help you differentiate between the simple issues and the more difficult ones. This will hopefully prevent overcomplicating those Mitzvahs that can be done quickly and easily and still have enormous impact on the lives of others.

One additional note: The Tzedakah principles and procedures I describe are relevant not only to individual giving, but also to companies and corporations, schools, and foundations.

Personalized Tzedakah: An Historical Note

Gym Shoes and Irises was my first book about Tzedakah, published in 1982. As I was putting the finishing touches on the manuscript, my publisher, Alvin Schultzberg, founder of The town House Press, suggested adding two words to the title — *Personalized Tzedakah*. He was right, absolutely right, and these two words describing my approach to giving have stood the test of time. The phrase captured both aspects of my writing: (1) that your Tzedakah work should touch you personally on a very profound level, and (2) that the beneficiaries of your Tzedakah should always be seen as real-live people. To elaborate:

1. Over the years, as I continued to write about this glorious Mitzvah, I began to understand more profoundly how intimately Tzedakah is tied to Life. Everywhere I saw Tzedakah happening, I discovered yet another Tzedakah/Life

connection. Tzedakah was "all about" the *gift* of Life, the very *fact* of being alive, and even how, by acts of Tzedakah, we *define* ourselves as human *beings*. With that ever-growing awareness, came a deep sense of joy, fulfillment, and meaning. The most sublime emotions emerged in those engaged in Tzedakah. Among them were those that the late Rabbi Abraham Joshua Heschel, ז״ל, emphasized so often in his teaching — awe, wonder, and radical amazement. That was one aspect of personalized Tzedakah.

2. Personalized Tzedakah also means that the beneficiary is a human being. Both giver and beneficiary share that common element, and any de-personalization would, therefore, be unacceptable. This explains terminology like "lonely people", "persons with disabilities", and "hungry individuals" instead of "*the* lonely", "*the* disabled", "*the* hungry". And it explains why a person doing Tzedakah should always keep in mind that it is human beings that a Tzedakah group or organization serves. The group or organization itself is of secondary importance.

This book, then, is offered as a *practical* guide to discovering more and better ways for you to deepen this personalization, which is the essence of Tzedakah, which is our intimate connection to Life.

Concluding Wishes and Blessings

In many ways, Tzedakah helps define us as Jews and as human beings. As my teacher, Rabbi Bradley Shavit Artson, has written, "Tzedakah is not about giving; Tzedakah is about being."

Tzedakah really is the Life-force, for both the beneficiaries of Tzedakah and for yourself. I hope you will find this guide useful for your own Tzedakah work.

לחיים-*Lechaim* – to Life! and נזכה למצוות-*Nizkeh LeMitzvot* — may we all have the privilege of a Lifetime of Tzedakah, Mitzvahs, and Tikkun Olam!

Will You Find "The Meaning of Life" by Doing Tzedakah?

I am convinced that the sense of meaning grows not by spectacular acts but by quiet deeds day by day.　　　　Rabbi Abraham Joshua Heschel, ז״ל

You might.

Many people have.

What is certain, however, is that you will know that there *is* meaning in your life when you have fed a hungry person that very day or for a week or a month into the future.

And that this person — for any one of a number of reasons — cannot afford to feed himself or herself.

And that the meals you are providing are tasty according to *their* own personal tastes, nutritious, and Menschlich.

There is no doubt that your act of Tzedakah has given vital sustenance to someone who might otherwise have wasted away. That Mitzvah you have done should also shift your own sense of what it means to be a human being into some higher realm. *You*, an "anybody" on the earth, used your money and saved a life. *That* is amazing, awesome. You have become more than just #2,476,551 in a census, or a tax paying-resident of Cook County, Illinois, or the sister of Jacob Levinson. You are *really* someone.

The same is true when you subsidize a dozen therapy sessions for someone whose life is unbearable.

I would think that this act of Tzedakah has profound significance for that other person who now has some hope…and unquestionably this also means so much *to you*.

You made it happen.

You changed the world by changing the life of one individual.

It is possible that you will build on these individual acts.

Because of what you have done, you may find yourself seeing things in a new light. What may happen is bi-directional, namely: (1) If you are now thinking constantly about Tzedakah, you may find yourself looking for new opportunities to do Good Things, and (2) as you gauge your daily — even mundane — activities, you will notice how many more of them can be tied into acts of Tzedakah. What happens may be a gradual process, or it may come in a sudden flash of insight. The end result *could* lead you to a general sense of spiritual serenity and wellbeing.

I believe that the search for The Meaning of Life is a good thing. I would never belittle the search itself nor minimize the *need* to search. I believe it is a most worthwhile human endeavor. However, I also believe that engaging in Tzedakah *during* the search may appreciably ease the restlessness and anxiety of the entire process.

Human beings want to feel that this thing, this gift called Life has depth, breadth, and a "feel" of awe-inspiring value. Jewish tradition teaches that money *can* become the ideal instrument for finding true, deep meaning. This is particularly curious, since money is so commonly maligned as the tool of greed and egocentricity.

Yes, you might possibly find The Meaning of Life through your Tzedakah. At the very least you will find more meaning in your own life.

One last thought: Will you find The Meaning of Happiness and at the same time *be* happy?

You will.

Most certainly you will.

What Are the Most Important *Jewish* Terms You Need to Know in Order to Do Tzedakah *Jewishly?*

There are a few essential terms you need to know to do your Tzedakah *Jewishly*: מצוה-Mitzvah, צדקה-Tzedakah, גמילות חסדים-Gemillut Chassadim, תיקון עולם-Tikkun Olam, and כבוד-Kavod.

מצוה-Mitzvah has two essential meanings: "commandment" and "good deed". Except as otherwise specified, in this book I am referring to the latter definition.

צדקה-Tzedakah, from the Hebrew root צ-ד-ק means "justice, doing the right thing", and is used primarily in this book to refer to using your money for the benefit of others. This term will be explained in greater detail throughout this guide. I also refer to a "צדיק-Tzaddik (m)/צדקת-Tzadeket (f)", meaning "Good Person, a man/woman who does Tzedakah".

גמילות חסדים-Gemillut Chassadim refers to physical acts of caring lovingkindness, i.e., using your time, talents, energy, and efforts (volunteering) for תיקון עולם-Tikkun Olam, fixing the world in any and every way possible. Clearly, both Tzedakah and Gemillut Chassadim are crucial elements for making complete Tikkun Olam happen. However, my focus in this guide is on the part the enormous power money has to change the world. In no way do I wish to imply that your time, energy, and effort are of secondary importance. A thorough study of Gemillut Chassadim may be found in my book *Who, Me? Yes, You! — Danny Siegel's Workbook to Help You Decide Where, When, Why, and How You Can Do Your Best Tikkun Olam.*

כבוד-Kavod means "dignity", "self-dignity", "human dignity", a vital element in all acts of Tzedakah. There is always a need to preserve not only the dignity of the recipient, but also of the giver. The issue of Kavod extends even to our use of other words and phrases. For example, using terms such as "*the* poor" or "*the* disabled" has an element of de-personalization. Individuals become categories of people. Phrases such as "individuals in need" and "persons with disabilities" would be the preferred terms. Similarly, "politically correct" vocabulary is an attempt to provide the most sensitive terms for various types or classes of human beings.

One additional word that I use frequently in this guide is "מענטשלעך-Menschlich". The Yiddish term "Mensch", meaning "a decent, caring, giving person", is used so frequently today by journalists, it is "almost English". "Menschlich", the adjectival form, can be combined with food, housing, and a general lifestyle. Thus, using your Tzedakah money to provide for hungry individuals should include enough dollars not only for the bare essentials, but also for "Menschlich" food. In other words, it should be the same amount of and kind of food you, yourself, would eat. "Menschlich housing" means "a *decent* place to live", i.e., a place that is nice enough to feel like a home to its occupants.

Once you know these terms well enough and feel sufficiently at ease to use them, you will be better able to *function* Jewishly when you are making your Tzedakah decisions. These are more than just words. They represent Jewish *values*, and, while they may overlap in some ways with concepts of giving from the secular world and from other religions, there are important distinctions. The more you actually *do* your Tzedakah *Jewishly*, the clearer the similarities and distinctions will become.

The Basic Principles
of Tzedakah

What Is the Difference Between "Tzedakah", "Charity", and "Philanthropy"?

While all three terms refer to providing for others, by examining the origins of the words, you will recognize that there are significant differences. It is true that there are areas that overlap. However, the unique practice of "Tzedakah" becomes evident when you examine where their meanings diverge.

"Charity" comes from the word "caritas", the Latin word for "love".

"Philanthropy" is composed of two Greek elements: the "phil" part means "love", and the "anthropy" (from *anthropos*) means "man", "love of man". (In the 21st century, we would say, "love of humanity".)

"Tzedakah" (and its intimately-related term "Tzedek") comes from the ancient Hebrew root "צדק", meaning "justice", "the right thing to do". As I see it, one advantage of the term "Tzedakah" is that, if it is your starting point for giving, it is extremely easy to find things that are wrong in the world which you can make right by doing Tzedakah. In fact, you may not be a particularly "loving person", but you can still do Tzedakah. Or you may find a situation where someone you don't love or don't even like is in need, and you will still do something for that person's benefit.

In addition, in several passages in Biblical literature "Tzedek" and "Tzedakah" mean "victory". The implication is clear: The good and the right *ultimately* win out in the world and in Life. In the broadest, almost cosmic sense, these terms mean that all the world's problems are *ultimately* solvable by acts of Tzedakah. As my teacher, Rabbi Arthur Green has translated the words of the famous Chassidic Rebbi, Rabbi Nachman of Bratzlav, "Despair is not an option-אין שום יאוש בעולם כלל".

And, furthermore, according to some Biblical philologists, "Tzedek" and "Tzedakah" can also be translated as "success". This is surely a most powerful re-definition for anyone who is looking to be "successful" in life.

What Are "Mitzvah Heroes", and Why Are They Such a Critical Part of Our Quest to Give Our Money Away?

As you read this guide, I write about trust and reliability as the most important issues to consider when deciding where to contribute your Tzedakah money. Since Mitzvah heroes personify trustworthiness and reliability, it is important to explain what I mean by the term "Mitzvah hero". The following is based on my experience of more than three decades working with more than 200 of these remarkable human beings.

Mitzvah heroes are giants of Tikkun Olam. They are experts in this field because they are intensely involved in changing lives by small, medium, and large Mitzvah-deeds. It is *because of their Tikkun Olam work* that they have a profound understanding of the essence of caring, power-as-Mitzvah-power, and the nature of people as human beings. Many seem to have been born with a deep sensitivity to the needs of others and *to respond by their actions* directly and powerfully to those needs. Others developed and refined their latent Tikkun Olam sensibilities and skills as they continued their holy work.

Mitzvah heroes are men and women of all ages, intelligence, educational background, religious affiliation, and economic status. Some see themselves as destined from birth for this kind of Grand Endeavor, and others still express surprise at themselves for having taken this path in life. All of them are inspired and inspiring and delightful to be with, individuals of the highest personal integrity, *absolutely* trustworthy, and all of them have one concern and one concern alone: that the lives of other people *should* and *can* be made better by their actions. People who meet them are universally struck by how *authentic* they are. Mitzvah heroes are the best-of-the-best human beings they have ever met.

For these reasons alone, your search for worthy recipients of your Tzedakah money should begin with Mitzvah heroes and their Tikkun Olam work.

But, there are additional reasons to begin with Mitzvah heroes. None of them is comfortable with the label, "Mitzvah hero", but they *are* willing to be known as teachers. They are, indeed, the best teachers of Mitzvahs, Tzedakah, and Tikkun Olam. If it is the very nature of "Mitzvah hero-ness" to be Tikkun Olam teachers, then we ought to learn about them and their work, meet them, spend our time with them, work with them, and, as a consequence of the *doing*, learn from them…and most definitely support them with your Tzedakah money. To analogize: For those looking for the right graduate school, a student looks for two things — the right kind of program *and* certain specific professors who are the best in their field. A master's in drama, might lead you to two choices — a program that stresses academics, or one that teaches everything about hands-on acting, playwriting, and the art and mechanics of stage design and lighting. Having chosen which *kind* of drama program is best, the student then has to pick the program where the right professor for his or her own specific needs is teaching. Certainly, then, if the field of endeavor is Fixing the World, What Makes Good People Good, Life Itself, and the Meaning of Life, the wise decision would be for you to meet Mitzvah heroes, and to learn to do Tikkun Olam the way they do it. You, then, carry those lessons further and do your own kind of Tikkkun Olam.

For some people (myself included), Mitzvah heroes may even have the answer to the question, "What is the meaning of life?". Their answer: Life is Mitzvahs. The Mitzvah hero might state it in different words, such as, "Some people first want to understand all of the 'Why of It All' and then to act. It is really the other way around. First of all, you *do*: *You* hold the hand of the lonely person; *you* spoon-feed an Elder who can no longer feed herself or himself, *you* pay a scholarship at a swimming pool or for therapeutic horseback riding lessons for someone damaged by a stroke so he or she can have a better chance at 100% rehabilitation. You *do* those things, and *after* you have done them, *then* you will have a better understanding of the 'Why of It All'. If you ask and ask and spend years asking, you may have missed out." This is just one of the many lessons to be absorbed when working with and supporting Mitzvah heroes.

Throughout this book, I refer to several of my own Mitzvah heroes. You will become familiar with names like Anita Shkedi, PK Beville, Dr. William Thomas, Ray Buchanan, Joseph Gitler, Kathy Freund, and Avshalom Beni. Their work — as well as that of 100 of my other Mitzvah heroes — is described in the Annual Reports" section of my Ziv Tzedakah Fund website, **www.ziv.org**. You, yourself, most likely already know some Mitzvah heroes, and will discover others through your own research and Tikkun Olam work. The end result will most certainly be a more refined, efficient, extensive, and meaningful use of your Tzedakah money.

What Is The Difference Between "Tzedakah" and "Fundraising", and What Exactly Is a "Non-Profit"?

"Tzedakah-צדקה" refers to using your money for the benefit of others. The Hebrew root of Tzedakah is צ-ד-ק-TZ-D-K, which means "justice". You would give Tzedakah because it is the right thing to do. This term is discussed in greater detail in separate chapters of this guide.

"Fundraising" is one aspect of Tzedakah. It applies to some, but not all, Tzedakah situations. Tzedakah fundraising may include a Jewish day school raising money for scholarships, community efforts to benefit people who have suffered greatly in a natural disaster, and friends who have decided to launch an e-mail campaign for a child needing a life-saving operation that costs $200,000. Your own Tzedakah money may be a part of such a campaign, but Tzedakah also includes all those personalized acts you may do when you donate your money. Buying the necessary tools for an unskilled immigrant worker is Tzedakah, as is paying the mortgage for someone who is about to lose a home because personal illness has made him or her lose a job. These are your own acts of doing what is right and just and good, with or without a larger campaign.

In addition, "fundraising" has developed its own set of rules and techniques. Most of these are effective and appropriate, though not necessarily universally so. For example, there is a famous "90-10 Rule" for large campaigns, namely, that 90% of the money comes from 10% of the donors. While that is often true, there are exceptions. When you contribute your Tzedakah money, you should determine whether or not — for that particular effort — it is the right approach. Mass mailings and media advertisements are other forms of fundraising. For these modes of raising funds, you will want to learn more about the fundraising expenses compared to the amount of money raised.

A "non-profit" is a tax-exempt, non-profit, corporation in the Internal Revenue Service Code. The most common type of non-profit you will encounter is a "501(c)(3)", which refers to the specific section of the IRS code. Donors to a 501(c)(3) are entitled to deduct their donation from their taxes, a great advantage both to the non-profit organization and to the donor. There are thousands upon thousands of non-profits in the United States. In fact, legal 501(c)(3) status may be granted to a very broad range of organizations. Some groups engage in what might be called "classic Tzedakah", i.e., providing for the immediate and long-term needs of America's poor people. Other non-profits, though, may be fundraising mechanisms for the symphony, museums, environmental programs, or the preservation of historic battlefields, monuments, and homes or libraries of former Presidents. Whatever their objective, the same principle applies: The fact that an organization has attained non-profit status does not necessarily guarantee that the organization's managers and officers are making use of donations efficiently or wisely. Several chapters in this guide will help you assess which ones may be appropriate recipients of your Tzedakah money, and which ones may not be.

You will want to train yourself to spot Tzedakah scams. Hoaxes get considerable coverage in the media. As important, though, is your research into *legitimate* non-profits. You will always want to check out "the numbers": Are salaries, fundraising, and infrastructure expenses eating away an unreasonably high percentage of your Tzedakah dollar? Inefficiency, waste, and mismanagement are much more common than outright fraud. Other sections of this book will provide specific guidelines for assessing a non-profit's use of the money at its disposal.

One other note concerning the term "non-profit": Organizations that are non-profits in other countries, including Israel, do not necessarily entitle you to a tax deduction in the United States. They must also be incorporated as a 501(c)(3) with the IRS for you to get a deduction. Many organizations have associated groups such as "American Friends of...", which indicates that they *are* tax-exempt in the U.S., though you will also want to examine *their* finances to learn about their own overhead and management practices

Why Give Tzedakah at All?

הנה תאבתי לפקדיך בצדקתך חיני

I love your Mitzvahs.
Give me Life through Your Tzedakah.   Psalm 119:40

Life is a short-term interest-bearing loan. Tikkun Olam is the interest you
pay.   Professor Eliezer Jaffe, Tzedakah Rebbi to the author

Many of our classic texts teach that a Jew should do Mitzvahs because they are just that — Mitzvahs. They are God's commandments, guiding us through this precious gift called "Life" and filling our days, hours, and moments with meaning. In some sense, they are intended to show us how our years, days, hours, and even our moments may best be appreciated and put to holy use. One of the first instructions God gives to Abraham is:

כי ידעתיו למען אשר יצוה את־בניו ואת־ביתו אחריו
ושמרו דרך יהוה לעשות צדקה ומשפט

For I have selected him [Abraham]
so that he may instruct his children and his posterity after him
to keep God's ways: to do what is just and right [Tzedakah U'Mishpat]
                    Genesis 18:19

Furthermore, Jewish tradition takes the position that our *deeds* form our thoughts, and not the other way around. It is by *doing* that we form our attitudes; the way we act has the power to bring us to an intellectual and spiritual appreciation for the sanctity of Life.

Finally, our tradition demonstrates a deep understanding of human motivations. Human beings — *because* they are human — are not always capable of behavior inspired by such lofty motives. One text makes this abundantly clear:

דאמר רב יהודה אמר רב:
לעולם יעסוק אדם בתורה ובמצות אף על פי שלא לשמה
שמתוך שלא לשמה – בא לשמה

Rav Yehuda said in the name of Rav:

A person should always engage in Torah and Mitzvahs even if they don't
do them for their own sake, because — even if the person engages in them
not for their own sake — eventually the person will do them for their own
sake.
                    Pesachim 50b

Your own motives for giving Tzedakah may differ from "Mitzvahs are Mitzvahs, and Jews are supposed to do Mitzvahs". What follows is a more detailed review of some of the many other possible conscious or unconscious reasons for your generosity:

Accomplishment I: You may like the sense of accomplishment. Giving Tzedakah is, for lack of a better term, very "real". You have not only thought about or theorized about "the significance of action" in a philosophical context, but you have also *done* something, some Mitzvah, that you can actually *feel*. That act of Tzedakah touches Life, the world *outside* of yourself, *and* your *internal* being. Your sense of accomplishment is rooted in the feeling that you are not helpless in the face of the ostensibly insurmountable troubles, sadness, and human woe in the world. You *can* change lives for the better.

Accomplishment II: Think of the many times you have said "This made my day." You can pinpoint some moment that stood out as having greater significance than all of the other moments of the day. It may well be that some weird circumstance "makes your day". For example, your distant cousin, two years younger than yourself has been called to Paradise. Totally unexpectedly, a codicil to the will states, "...and I leave my 17-room mansion in Westchester and every nickel in my on-shore and off-shore bank accounts to my dear cousin Heschie." Total value: $43,000,000 after all taxes are paid. And this is the cousin you used to taunt with nicknames like "fatty" or "doofus". In fact, it was perfect timing, as you were close to actually leaving the job you have hated for 10 years, even though no new employment opportunities were on the horizon. I suppose that kind of thing would "make your day", though the odds of that actually happening are approximately slim-to-zero. On the other hand, giving Tzedakah has the ability to "make your day" every time you do it.

"Connectedness": You feel connected. With an act of Tzedakah you are neither alone nor lonely. You are attached to others — to other human beings who share your common human sense of fear, sadness, pain, *and* joy. You are linked to others wherever they may be on the face of the earth. You are attached to the past, because for more than three millennia Jewish tradition has taught that this is how you should respond to the needs of others. You are linked to the present, because you are doing something for others that happens *now*. *And* you are a part of their future, whether it is the kid who has no family who goes to camp because of your Tzedakah money or the infant car seat you provided to a single mother who has no money to buy one. Whatever the specific situation, your future and theirs are forever bound one to another.

Power: You are aware of how power *can* be abusive and *is* abused. Leafing through even a few pages of a newspaper or catching three minutes on the nightly news causes you distress. Simultaneously, you know that the right kind of power *can* be a great human blessing. You may feel that in your heart, mind, and soul, and *in your bones*. Any thoughts of being helpless or trapped have been dismissed from your mind. You *can* change the way things are.

Self-image: The prior descriptions make you feel good about yourself. You know you are *somebody* because your acts of Tzedakah have done so much for others. Social workers and every kind of therapist are often called upon to work with individuals who have lost their self-image. These specialists have developed many fine methods for dealing with a person's broken, battered, suppressed, or lost self-esteem. Every day, the therapists build and re-build their clients' bruised self-image. Time and again, the same holds true for concerned classroom teachers, camp counselors, and sports coaches. Each one, in turn, uses his or her own skills to allow the patients, students, players, wards, and campers to develop fully as human beings with a solid, stable, and resilient feeling of self-worth. Giving Tzedakah can serve as a constant reminder that you *are* someone of value.

I would certainly add Mitzvah heroes to the list of healers. These are individuals who, through their grand Tzedakah work teach, train, and encourage others to become Mitzvah People. As mentioned throughout this book, Mitzvah heroes are distinguished teachers in the field of Tzedakah, Mitzvahs, and Tikkun Olam. They know intimately how very great the power of Tzedakah is to remind others that they *are* somebody. And not only that they are *somebody*, but somebody of great value both to themselves as well as to others. Tzedakah opportunities are so numerous and varied, Mitzvah heroes *know* that there is an appropriate match for every individual. And just as a therapist designs a plan of treatment according to the needs of each individual patient, so, too, Mitzvah heroes use their skills to make the best possible match. Whatever scale is used to measure improvement in self-image, empirical studies demonstrate that Tzedakah is extremely effective.

Stability: It is true that some people thrive on chaos. Biographies and autobiographies of many artists, musicians, authors, and poets give eloquent testimony to that fact-of-Life. You may simply need stability in your life. You are not extreme about this and don't display any characteristics of being a control freak. However, some degree of order and orderliness allows you to function well. Giving Tzedakah, as well as doing Deeds of Goodness and Kindness with your time *can* bring order out of chaos. This is particularly true if you have established a regular habit of giving.

Meaning in Life: Giving Tzedakah might possibly give meaning to your life. For a full discussion of this area of giving, see the chapter *Will I find "The Meaning of Life" by doing Tzedakah?*

Feeling Good: Earlier in this chapter I mentioned "feeling good about yourself" and how giving Tzedakah may lead you to that frame of mind. I think that there is an even more basic feeling which Tzedakah touches very deeply: just plain feeling good. Your ability to feel good about yourself depends on genetics, accident, upbringing, environment, happenstance, possible psychosomatic elements, and a mile-long list of other factors. The same is true for your "unhappiness threshold". What is clear, however, is that you would prefer to feel good rather than bad. Giving Tzedakah most definitely can be a contributing factor to good feelings. The Talmud records an interesting statement by Rabbi Yehoshua ben Levi:

אמר רבי יהושע בן לוי...

חש בגרונו...חש במעיו...חש בעצמותיו...חש בכל גופו...חש בראשו —
יעסוק בתורה

If you have a headache…, a sore throat…, a stomach ache…, a pain in your bones…, pain in your entire body — study Torah.   Eruvin 54a

Many interpretations have been given, some medically and psychologically valid, others rather far-fetched. Two excellent comments I have heard are that (1) studying Torah takes your mind off your pain, and (2) because Torah study is of such great importance to you, it can elevate you above your pain. I would think that what is true for Torah study would certainly be true for giving Tzedakah. As you do your Tzedakah giving, many "Woe is me!" thoughts can fade into the back of your consciousness. Though you do not feel *well* because of some physical pain, you can still feel *good*.

To summarize: On the one hand, Mitzvahs are Mitzvahs, and doing them for sublime reasons is a most worthy approach. In the final analysis, however, any and all of the other motivations produce great benefits for both the recipient *and* the giver, and that *really* is what is most important. The world is a better place; people in need feel better; they have food, warmth, a roof over their heads, and they live with greater dignity — all because of the power of the Mitzvah of Tzedakah. And *you*, by using your Tzedakah money wisely, most definitely also feel very good. It is a true win-win life situation.

Did the Rabbis from Ancient and Medieval Times *Really* Understand "Real Life" When They Established the Rules for Giving Tzedakah?

כל האיברים תלוין בלב והלב תלוי בכיס

Every part of the human body depends on the heart,
But the heart depends on the pocket.　　　　　　Jerusalem Talmud, Terumot 8:10

א"ר יוחנן כיפה של חשבונות היתה חוץ לירושלים
וכל מי שמבקש לחשב הולך לשם
למה שלא יחשב בירושלים ויצר
לפי שנקרא משוש כל הארץ

Rabbi Yochanan said:
The arcade of [Jerusalem's] accountants' offices was outside the city limits of Jerusalem.
Whoever wanted to review his or her accounts would go there.
Why [were the accountants' offices outside of the city]?
In case a person would become depressed while reviewing the accounts —
[and being depressed would contradict the very nature of Jerusalem]
which is called "The Joy of the Entire Earth."
　　　　　　Exodus Rabba, end of Pekuday, Psalm 48:3

Did the Rabbis "get" how life is *really* lived, or were they so caught up in their Torah studies that they had lost touch with the "ordinariness" of daily living? Two Jewish texts written above should give us some insight:

It is easy to be lyrical about the amazing power of Tzedakah. Tzedakah done in the correct way elicits words and half-words that are heavily charged with emotion. "Awesome", "incredible!", "Ah!", and "Wow!" are only three of the reactions you may have when you watch Tzedakah work its wonders. That is how it should be. The poetic level of Tzedakah allows you to not only *know* but also to *feel* that life can be very rich and beautiful. Yet, you live your life day-to-day, hour-by-hour, and minute-by-minute, and most of your time is extremely prosaic. The first text in this chapter is a very realistic reminder that, without money, you cannot even have the most basic essentials you need to live. The heart — seat of emotions, personality, aspirations, and dreams — simply won't function unless there is money in the pocket to feed, provide warmth for, and shelter your human body.

Similarly, it is easy to be lyrical about ירושלים-Jerusalem. It is the City of Holiness, capital of our Jewish homeland, a geographical point that is more than just another place on the map. Jerusalem is also known in our tradition as משוש כל הארץ-The Joy of the Entire World. (Psalm 48:3) As strange as it sounds, the implication is that you are *required* to be joyous when you are in Jerusalem. I know that there are people who say you can't *force* people to feel a certain way, but the fact is that Rabbi Yochanan thought that you could. To analyze the story:

1. On the one hand, Rabbi Yochanan was fully aware of Jerusalem's awe-inspiring character.

2. He also knew the great impact paying bills and the rising cost of a liter of milk has on your emotions and consciousness. Holiness is one thing; putting food on the table and keeping your family warm in the chilly, rainy winter in The Holy City is another.

3. Rabbi Yochanan wanted to make certain that living the high spiritual life was a good thing...as long as it was understood that sooner or later you would have to make your way to the accountant's office to keep yourself realistically rooted in "real" life.

4. Even then, Rabbi Yochanan teaches us — do your accounts, worry about numbers and financial stability, but remember that you are going home. When you are back within the city limits, keep some perspective. Live the moment-to-moment with all its mundane concerns; just know that beyond, above, and all around you is a city of holiness and joy.

Does Tzedakah Money Really Belong to You?

קונם כהנים ולוים נהנים לי יטלו על כרחו

[If a farmer says,] "I vow that the כהנים-*Kohanim, Priests and* לוים-*Levi'im, Levites should have no benefit of anything that is mine, they may still take, even against the farmer's will.*　　Mishnah Nedarim 11:3

In Biblical times, farmers had certain obligations to use a part of their crops for Tzedakah. Among the types of Mitzvah-produce designated for poor people were:

לקט-Leket, gleanings
פאה-Pe'ah, the corners of the field
שכחה-Shichecha, areas the farmer forgot to reap.

In addition, there were special portions set aside for the Priests and Levites:

תרומה-Terumah for the Priests
מעשר-Ma'aser for the Levites.

Some of the rules of distribution and their underlying principles includes:

1. Even if the farmer solemnly vows not to give Terumah and Ma'aser, the Kohanim and Levi'im can *still* take the Terumah and Ma'aser, because they *rightfully* belong to them. This is clearly stated in the Mishnah at the beginning of this chapter.
1. This means that Terumah and Ma'aser never really belonged to the farmer.
1. Consequently, the farmer cannot *not* give them to the Kohanim and Levi'im.
1. In certain situations, the farmer may designate *which* Kohanim and Levi'im may receive the Terumah and Ma'aser.
1. No matter which specific Kohanim or Levi'im the farmer designates, it still *must* be set aside.
1. The farmer is not even allowed to use the rest of the crop for personal needs until the Terumah and Ma'aser have been set aside,

Other Jewish texts support this position concerning what you really own and what you do not own. Tzedakah money doesn't belong to you to begin with, and rather than viewing yourself as sharing what you own, you are asked to understand that you are a trustee — God's trustee — over this percentage of your money. As a trustee, agent, and partner-with-God, you therefore have the sacred duty to live up to your obligation to distribute your Tzedakah money wisely. On the one hand, it is an awesome, perhaps overpowering thought to be God's partner. It is certainly very humbling. But on the other hand, it is very empowering to know that there is a distinctly Divine element in the act of Tzedakah.

Thus, in Jewish life, there really are two kinds of money — money for your own personal use, and Tzedakah money, which is money to be used for the good of other people.

Many questions that apply to your own money also apply to Tzedakah. The two most crucial questions are:

1. "Yours" — How much money do you require for *your* personal needs?
2. "Theirs" — How much Tzedakah money do *they* need?

The more you think of "yours" and "theirs", the more you will observe different categories of people and how they relate to money.

1. "Yours" — In the extreme, some people live as if there is never enough money in their account and always crave more. They may consider a 10-room house on five acres of land insufficient for a two-person household. A friend of mine once called this "living large".
1. "Theirs" — At the other end of the people-and-money scale, some people never stop wanting more Tzedakah money to accomplish that much more Tikkun Olam. Instead of having X dollars to distribute, they wish that they had 10 times X Tzedakah dollars or X to the 10th power of Tzedakah dollars at their disposal. They "live large" through their giving, insisting on doing the Mitzvah with an extra-generous touch. This is known as "הידור מצוה-Hiddur Mitzvah", Doing a Mitzvah Beautifully.
1. "Yours and theirs" — Another one of my friends said it succinctly and eloquently, "If you *live* large, *give* large."

The distance between the two extremes is very great. Most people are somewhere in the middle.

1. You may know a few people who are so successful that they have a winter beachfront mansion on Maui and a ski chalet in Utah who still want more and more and always more. You have certainly observed their lifestyles in the media, but most likely, they are not your "main crowd". There is even a slight chance that you, yourself, are one of the "never enough" people.
1. You may be fortunate to know several people who have a private jet, $3,000 suits, and a landscape architect on retainer to re-design their grounds at their slightest whim — but who are generous-to-the-extreme (in the most positive sense) with their Tzedakah money. They *live* large and *give* large. You may be one yourself. You are *living* large and *giving* large.
1. You may be one of those who *doesn't* happen to book the penthouse suite at the Plaza Hotel in New York or doesn't happen to have umteen thousands of shares of stock in your portfolio. You may be just plain old middle class, living well within your means while worrying about meeting the next college tuition payment for your daughter. *But* you consciously and frequently let your mind wander to thoughts like, "If I only had $10,000,000 for Tzedakah." Good. That's a very healthy approach to "yours" and "theirs" money.

To conclude this chapter, I would add two practical items to the list:

1. Find some useful short quote that you can memorize that will allow you to be constantly aware of the "yours" and "theirs" of money. I personally think that Winston Churchill's quote is one of the best: "We make a living by what we get, but we make a life by what we give."
1. Calculate where you are at present on this "yours" and "theirs" scale, and every so often review the results. Make a note of all the changes that have occurred over time.

Most of all, whatever you do — do as much of "theirs" as you can.

What Does It Mean "to Do Tzedakah *Jewishly*"?

Judaism offers many ways to do Tzedakah. Several of the principles, values, techniques, and strategies are unique to Jewish tradition. In addition, while it is true that some of the fundamental concepts may have elements common to other systems of giving, Judaism places a different emphasis on those concepts. Furthermore, the organic and dynamic interplay of the Jewish concepts with *acts* of Tikkun Olam provides a distinct approach to discovering the real needs of others. The *Jewish* way of giving becomes most evident when you examine *exactly* how these needs are to be met.

"Doing Tzedakah *Jewishly*" involves two essential elements: (1) Giving your money away according to distinctly Jewish values and guidelines, and (2) your actual Tzedakah decisions, i.e., how much you give to Jewish programs and how much to general programs.

1. Unique Jewish values and practices relating to Tzedakah are discussed throughout this guide. Jewish guidelines for proper Tzedakah giving are as necessary to a civilized, ordered society as traffic laws, fire codes, and fair rental contracts. Tzedakah directives are established to allow you, the giver, to be more efficient in your desire to benefit others. You should be able to easily integrate Jewish practices into contemporary life, American laws, and the latest electronic tools such as e-mail and the internet. Most important, once you are familiar with Judaism's procedures and rules, you will find that there is vast room for individuality and creativity in your own giving. You can work behind the scenes, "on the front lines", or do some combination of both. Whichever way you do it, you should *never* have reason to doubt that you are making a difference.

2. Thousands of years of Jewish experience should offer guidance as you consider how much to give to Jewish needs and how much to needs beyond the Jewish community. Among several factors to consider are:

> A. Jewish tradition does not provide an absolute, easy-to-follow "chart" which outlines, "12% to this category of needs, 9% to that type of program, etc." For example, some texts teach that Tzedakah's first priority is saving lives. Other passages in traditional Jewish literature give precedence to local needs in contrast to those far away. Still others stress the priority of Israel's needs, redeeming captives, supporting Torah study, as well as giving to Jewish and/or non-Jewish needs. All of these texts indicate that *their* recipients should be the most important beneficiaries of Tzedakah. I have found no clear text that ties all of these positions together and gives an authoritative list of "first priorities".

> B. Jewish tradition certainly allows and, indeed, encourages contributing to causes and needs beyond the Jewish community, as exemplified by the recent outpouring of funds for victims of

the September 11th attacks, the devastating hurricanes of 2005, and for the survivors of the Asian tsunami.

    C. It would be important to learn:

        (1) How much money *non-Jewish* organizations and individuals give to support *Jewish* needs.

        (2) It would also be helpful to review recent studies about the children and grandchildren of wealthy Jews who have inherited enormous sums of money. These studies reveal a disturbing trend: While the descendants may continue to contribute the same *absolute* amount of Tzedakah dollars as their parents or grandparents, they are giving significantly smaller percentages to Jewish needs. These factors should also help you determine how much Tzedakah from Jewish people is needed to provide for the needs of the Jewish community.

        (3) You will want to review the overall and the specific needs of the various organizations benefiting the Jewish community. As described elsewhere in this guide, for Jewish Tikkun Olam programs that particularly appeal to you, you will want to research how efficiently they accomplish their goals.

    D. The uniquely crucial needs of Israel and its people. In your own giving, you will want to consider how much your own support will make a difference.

Your Jewish Identity

Most likely, your own sense of Jewish identity will largely determine both to what degree you give Jewishly and how much you give to Jewish Tzedakah programs. However you identify with your Jewishness, it is important to remember that there is no need to feel defensive about giving to Jewish needs. Being Jewish, it is natural for you to care about your own, and to *act* to assure the wellbeing of your own. Native Americans are not defensive about supporting the needs of Native Americans. The same is true for African Americans and other ethnic, racial, or religious groups. While there are advocates of strictly universalistic giving, every group still donates to programs with which they have common ties. "Particularistic" Tzedakah is perfectly acceptable.

The following three quotes may help you articulate the suitability of your "particularistic" choices:

1. Solomon Schechter, one of the great Jewish scholars of the early 20th century, wrote, "We can no more have Jews without Judaism, than Judaism without Jews. We Jews have proven that we can survive difference, but not indifference."

2. In one of his sermons, my teacher, Rabbi Saul Teplitz, wrote, "Often, one finds a phrase on theater tickets that reads: 'Void if detached.' So, too, Jewish life becomes void when it is detached from the practices and principles of Judaism,

from synagogue and prayer, from Torah and study." Rabbi Teplitz and I have discussed this, and he most certainly agreed that his list should include "and doing Tzedakah as Jews and for Jews."

3. Finally, returning to our early classic Jewish sources, Hillel's famous words certainly come to mind:

הוא היה אומר אם אין אני לי מי לי וכשאני לעצמי מה אני

Reversing the order of Hillel's phrases, I translate:

> *"If I am only for myself, what am I?*
> *But if I am not for myself as well, who will be for me?"* Pirkay Avot, Chapter 2

To summarize: "Doing Tzedakah *Jewishly*" encompasses two important features: (1) You will want to absorb the unique Jewish material on Tzedakah by whatever method of study you do best. (2) How you understand your own Jewish identity will display itself in the practices and emphases of your own Tzedakah giving.

Is "God Helps Those Who Help Themselves" a Jewish Principle?

You often hear the phrase "God helps those who help themselves" during a discussion of Tzedakah. Frequently, the implication is that, if people would only work hard, they wouldn't need Tzedakah. Almost as frequently, some will even add "They should pull themselves up by their bootstraps".

I would like to examine this aspect of self-help not only from a factual point of view but also from a Jewish perspective — primarily because I have heard the idea expressed with subtle and not-too-subtle negative feelings. The tone of voice will give it away — a slightly patronizing resonance that implies, "I have helped myself fairly well through difficult times — everyone else should be able to do the same." And, unfortunately, sometimes these words are uttered by non-givers or minimal-givers.

Let us take a closer look at this approach to Tikkun Olam:

In reality, while there are people who *can* help themselves, there are many "classes" of people who *cannot* help themselves — people with Alzheimer's, people in periods of history like the Great Depression who searched for jobs when there were none to be had, individuals with such severe disabilities they cannot function on their own, children and adults lying in hospitals intubated and monitored and unable to pay their medical bills. That is barely the beginning of even "the short list".

The appropriate *Jewish* response would be: We must use our resources to assure their physical, emotional, and spiritual wellbeing. And as much as we would like it to be done exclusively by human acts of Gemilut Chassadim — acts of caring, lovingkindness — it frequently takes money, Tzedakah money, to make it happen.

There are others, of course, who might be able to "help themselves", but setbacks of every kind and every degree may have stalled them: Natural disaster has demolished all their worldly possessions, corrupt corporate officials have wiped out their retirement accounts, batterers have forced spouses and children to flee the home with nothing but the clothes on their backs, freak accidents have caused severe injury. Again, this is just the beginning of even "the short list".

The appropriate *Jewish* response would be: We must use our resources to assure their physical, emotional, and spiritual wellbeing and to work with them to re-establish their stability and their ability to function with some greater degree of independence. Many Tzedakah organizations are devoted to just that aspect of Tikkun Olam — job training agencies, "business clothing" groups that provide individuals with proper attire for job interviews, social workers at shelters for victims of domestic violence, youth workers dedicated to getting kids out of gangs. And as much as we would like it to be done by human acts of Gemilut Chassadim, acts of caring, lovingkindness, it often takes money, Tzedakah money, and occasionally large sums of Tzedakah money to make it happen.

Yet another category of people — perhaps the most difficult and troubling for others — needs to be considered. These are individuals-in-need who are unpleasant, "difficult people", sometimes even insufferable and obnoxious in their relationships with others. Feeling helpless when you extend your hand, you might naturally distance yourself from them. Here, too, there is a Jewish response, in two stages:

First, you should attempt to recall times when you may have been unresponsive or even nasty when others reached out to you. While professional therapists may be able to recognize the reasons for other people's behavior, non-professionals are incapable of doing a psychiatric evaluation of why other people act the way they do. We must deal with the immediate situation-at-hand of another human being in need. Reminding ourselves of our own less-than-perfect personality traits lays the groundwork for a practical solution by calling on our sense of רחמנות-Rachmanut, empathy to encourage us to respond in some fashion. It reminds us that there is no "we" and "they", but, rather, that we have something very much in common.

Secondly, you need to recognize that there are Mitzvah heroes everywhere, "specialists" who *are* capable of working with these extreme situations. They seem to have the magic human touch (though there is no "magic" to it). Their exceptional sensitivities, tied to tremendous Mitzvah skills, allows the Mitzvah hero to reach even the most difficult people who would curse or resist in the most distasteful manner any attempts anyone might make to bring them benefit. The practical solution, then, would be to place our Tzedakah money at the disposal of these Mitzvah heroes, allowing them to bring stability, functionality, and wellbeing to the people they serve.

What Is "The 4th-Grader Principle"?

After more than three decades of work as a Tzedakah educator, I am convinced that most Tzedakah giving can be understood and explained by any 4th grader. I estimate that the kids get as much as 80-90% of "what Tzedakah is all about" and how to do it right. I used to think that the youngest age was Bar and Bat Mitzvah because Bar and Bat Mitzvah people are accomplishing so many great things in the world of Tzedakah. However, lately I have come to understand that even nine-year-olds and 10-year-olds "get it" just as well.

They understand needs: They know that unhappy adults need to get away for a week-end so that they can psychologically re-group and rebuild, that a slow-learning student needs a tutor, and that people who are hungry need food. They just *know* that rather than throwing out leftover cafeteria food, it should be donated to programs feeding hungry people. They see and *feel* that more Elders die in nursing homes from loneliness than from disease or the "normal" course of aging.

They understand methods: They know that for many situations, the solution is incredibly simple. For example, if a ramp is needed so people using wheelchairs can read from the Torah — then build a ramp. (As Nike put it, "Just do it!") Hearing them say, "Why can't we do it this way?" is often a wake-up call to many adults who have a tendency to over-complicate Tzedakah.

They *do* understand the need for money to make things happen: 427 Passover food packages cost money, paying for taxis for Elders who no longer drive to visit the graves of their deceased spouses costs money, buying polish to manicure the fingernails of Elders in nursing homes, and, thereby, giving them a psychological boost, costs money.

They understand overhead: They know that if you are giving a dollar or five or ten to Tzedakah, you want as much of that Tzedakah money as possible to be used for the stated purpose. And they *do not* accept waste as, "Well, that's just the way things are."

They know about trustworthiness: Just as they have friends they trust and with whom they share their most intimate feelings, parents to rely on, teachers who recognize their unique nature and abilities — they know that people using Tzedakah money need to be equally trusted. And just as they would not want to hang out with other kids they don't like, they would not want to have their Tzedakah money handled by someone they don't trust.

They see through bad reasoning: The classic example is a 4th grader who gave the best response I have yet heard about why some hospitals would not allow a visiting dog program. Everyone else was giving the "real" reasons: allergies, cleanliness, diseases, control, etc. But, this 10-year-old said, "You can't have dogs in hospitals because there is a sign that says, 'No Dogs Allowed.'" Kids pick up on "You can't do it because you can't do it" reasoning and reject it. Then, more often than not, they just go ahead and do it.

They may not know all of the intricacies of specific laws, rules, codes, or regulations, but once they learn them, they are usually capable of integrating them into their Tzedakah thinking and proceed accordingly to accomplish what needs to be done. Take the example of the ramp mentioned above: once they know about the legally required angle of the ramp, the need for a protective railing, and similar regulations, they digest the facts, and proceed with their plan. The classic example is donating food. Once they read the Bill Emerson Good Samaritan Food Donation Act — which frees the donor from liability — they are capable of working out the logistics of pick-up times, sanitary and safe food containers, etc. with any food establishment.

And they most certainly know that anyone involved in Tzedakah work only because they are good at what they do, or because it is their job— but have no passion, idealism, or devotion to the people in need — should be working somewhere else.

There is much to learn from "the little kids". You may benefit from a consultation with them about the Tzedakah you are about to donate.

Shouldn't Your Primary Concern Be to Make the Systemic Changes
That Will Eliminate Those Very Conditions That Cause People to Be in Need?

And, Should Tzedakah Money Be Used *Only* for Systemic Change?

And, If Not, What Percentage Is Appropriate for Giving for Systemic Change?

The answer to the first question: Yes. To a certain extent.

For example, The Preamble to the American Constitution expresses the following lofty ideals of American democracy:

We the People of the United States, in Order to form a more perfect Union, establish Justice, insure domestic Tranquility, provide for the common defense, promote the general Welfare, and secure the Blessings of Liberty to ourselves and our Posterity, do ordain and establish this Constitution for the United States of America.

In order to make those ideals a reality in our lives, the system has to be not only constructed properly, but it must also work. When the system is sluggish or dysfunctional, then systemic change is crucial to the entire Tikkun Olam context. You only need to consider the far-reaching changes brought about by the Voting Rights Act, the Civil Rights Act, and the Americans with Disabilities Act. All of these required enormous efforts by many people as well as considerable financial resources.

The preceding paragraph describes aspects of the democratic system. Studying socialism, communism, feudalism, fascism and various societal experiments, for example, and comparing and contrasting them, will naturally sharpen your sense of how societies function, and whether or not — even if they function smoothly — they preserve human dignity. As productive, I would think, would be a review of the development and state of the kibbutz in Israel. Why and how kibbutzim were founded, how they developed, and how they dealt with and deal with aging populations, individuals with special needs, and their understanding of Tzedakah and Tikkun Olam is very enriching and would possibly contribute greatly to your own personal practice of Tzedakah.

So, yes, working for systemic change, and applying Tzedakah money towards that kind of change is of major importance. But another aspect of Tzedakah remains, the personalized i.e., "in the meantime..." type of Tzedakah. In the meantime, there are people without the most basic human shelter, access to essential health services — even something as simple as aspirin, who go days without food and have no hope for any in the immediate future. Not only does this kind of basic Tzedakah provide *immediate* relief, it often leads many people to find systemic solutions for those very needs that they have discovered when giving.

There are really two ways to arrive at systemic solutions: (1) theoretical thinking, whereby experts in societal structure and function study the system and then offer possible solutions for the world's ills, and (2) front-line Tzedakah work, which leads to creative all-encompassing change. In and of itself, neither approach is sufficient to bring us to a just and fair world. Both approaches complement each other. However, I sense that the better, more long-lasting solutions originate with Tzedakah work that is, as it were, in the trenches of mud, filth, mental confusion on either side of the line of madness, bone-chilling cold, and the rumbling stomachs of schoolchildren whether they are in Afula, Detroit, or Minsk who want to learn math, literature, and history but haven't had breakfast. A regular pattern of *personalized* Tzedakah that deals constantly with the needs of *real people* provides an everpresent reminder that you are involved in the lives of *human beings* with very *real* needs. Solutions demand a measure of childhood naïveté that sometimes sees the world without the muddling interference of over-intellectualizing. And, as well, solutions demand sophisticated adult reasoning, power, and ability to connect resources to needs. How much of which you, yourself, will use, depends on your own personality. Whatever you choose as best for yourself, once personalized, Tzedakah will saturate every aspect of your Mitzvah work. As a result, you may very well be led to a clearer vision of full, even ultimate, Tikkun Olam solutions.

Is There Enough Money to Do It, to Do It All?

ואמר רבי יצחק....
כל הרודף אחר צדקה
הקדוש ברוך הוא ממציא לו מעות ועושה בהן צדקה
רב נחמן בר יצחק אמר
הקדוש ברוך הוא ממציא לו בני אדם המהוגנים
לעשות להן צדקה

Rabbi Yitzchak said...:
The Holy One will provide sufficient money
for any who runs to do Tzedakah.
Rabbi Nachman bar Yitzchak said:
The Holy One will provide appropriate recipients
through whom to perform the Mitzvah of Tzedakah.   Bava Batra 9b

Rabbi Yitzchak's words reveal Judaism's optimistic approach to Tzedakah. If you are willing to take the first step with your money, you can be certain that you will find more money to do Tzedakah. Either others will be moved by your act of Tzedakah and will contribute, or you will find that you, yourselves, actually can manage to give away more than you had originally thought possible. Or both will happen.

Rabbi Nachman bar Yitzchak adds another encouraging element, namely, that your Tzedakah money will not go to waste. There are several techniques that you can learn in order to help you find the appropriate recipients. Most of them are no more difficult than how to turn on a TV or to make a bowl of instant oatmeal. These techniques constitute a significant portion of this guide.

The Practical Guide
to Giving Tzedakah

What Are Some Techniques for Raising Your Tzedakah Awareness?

The end of the calendar year is "high time" for Tzedakah donations. It is the last chance for donors to review their Tzedakah contributions for tax purposes. Some people do all of their Tzedakah at that time, but many are uncomfortable with this once-a-year method. They understand that because of a sudden cold wave in October, some immediate need has to be addressed, or they are aware that giving frequently during the course of the year gives them a sense of Tzedakah as a *regular* practice, part of their "normal" life. In no particular order, the following are a few suggestions for keeping Tzedakah in the forefront of both your Tzedakah thinking and your Tzedakah *doing*.

1. Tzedakah boxes (pushkas)

   A. Keep several Tzedakah boxes (pushkas) around your house. This will provide you with many more opportunities to *visually* remember to do Tzedakah.

   B. Keep a Tzedakah box near the washing machine for all the loose coins and the occasional bills that you might find in pockets.

   C. Periodically check under the cushions of couches and easy chairs. They are likely treasure troves of Tzedakah money.

   D. Empty your loose change at the end of the day into the pushka. One friend was delighted when his apartment building changed the washers and driers from quarters to a magnetic card. That "liberated" considerably more money — quarters galore — for his pushka.

   E. Periodically estimate by weight how much has accumulated. This stimulates yet another of the five senses to the importance of Tzedakah.

   F. At regular intervals, count the accumulated coins and bills. For the coins — resist the temptation to use a bank's automatic counting machine. Pouring all the coins into a machine in a huge rush and immediately reading the total on a screen tends to dull the sense of how coins add up to significant amounts of money for Tikkun Olam. Do it the old-fashioned way: Count everything slowly and carefully and roll them into packages to take to the bank.

   G. Every so often, create your own pushka. Some people prefer to make see-through Tzedakah boxes so that they can watch the Tzedakah money grow. Others prefer any material that prevents seeing how much has accumulated. They prefer the surprise and delight of the slowly-growing total as they sort and count the coins and bills.

H. Put other "found money", such as coins you might find on the sidewalk — in the pushka. The late Rabbi Richard Israel, ז״ל, was a long-distance runner. Every year, Ziv Tzedakah Fund would receive a check representing a sizable amount of money he had found during his hundreds of miles of jogging.

2. Put a reminder in your PDA to give Tzedakah some time every day. Choose your own best option: to flash on the screen periodically during the day, to have a sound alarm go off first thing in the morning, to design a graphic that will bring the message home to yourself. *Whatever works best for you.*

3. Holidays and Shabbat: Before lighting candles on Friday and before holidays, put some money in a Tzedakah box. Tying Tzedakah to this beautiful ritual of light can be very powerful; juxtaposing the two gives greater significance to both the sacred time of Shabbat-and-holidays *and* to Tzedakah.

- Purim has a special name for its specific Mitzvah of Tzedakah — Matanot LaEvyonim-מתנות לאביונים (Gifts to Poor People). On this particularly joyous and fun day, you would want to make sure that everyone can join in the fun, including having a fine holiday meal.

- Passover has two terms for its own Tzedakah, one in Hebrew and one in Aramaic: Ma'ot Chittin-מעות חטין, Money for Wheat and Kimcha DePischa-קימחא דפיסחא, [Money for] Passover Flour. Both of them mean "to donate money so that people who cannot afford Matzah will be able to have it".

- On Yom Kippur and other fast days, the money you would have spent on your own meals were you not fasting is to go to Tzedakah. As the Talmudic Rabbi Mar Zutra taught hundreds of years ago: אגרא דתעניתא צדקתא — the reward for fasting is Tzedakah. (Brachot 6b) I find the term "אגרא-agra", reward, a very interesting choice of words on Mar Zutra's part. Why a reward? I have heard several interpretations, one of which makes the most sense to me in the framework of Talmudic thinking: If fasting is meant as a vehicle to help you re-orient your sense of values, then Mar Zutra is saying, "*Prove* your new priorities by *doing* something for others." The "reward", then, would be that you have had the opportunity to do a Mitzvah.

D. Remembering to provide for others before *any* holiday is another way of making certain that Tzedakah is a frequent part of your cycle of living and giving.

4. Every time you go grocery shopping, buy one extra item for Tzedakah, and deliver the items regularly to the synagogue food box or other agencies' collection points.

5. Make two separate checking accounts, one for Tzedakah and one for personal expenses. Use different-colored checks, and sign both differently (possibly using a middle initial or some other device to remind yourself which is which).

6. As soon as you receive *any* income, separate the appropriate percentage for Tzedakah and deposit it in the Tzedakah bank account. From their earliest age, your children should also get into the habit of separating their money, whether from allowance, money received as presents, or jobs of any kind, no matter how little the amount they receive.

7. Hold regular family meetings to discuss various opportunities for giving. Make sure to listen to your children. They frequently have ideas and insights that you might miss completely.

8. Have get-togethers with friends to discuss the needs of others and where your individual or combined Tzedakah may best be used. Form a Tzedakah collective.

9. Read about, learn about, and talk about Tzedakah frequently. Create a physical file of newspaper and magazine articles about The Good People who are doing great Tikkun Olam work. Similarly, bookmark important Tikkun Olam websites for easy reference. Share the stories, lessons, and ideas with your family and circle of friends.

10. Daydream often.

>A. If it is a cloudy day, imagine seeing a humongous pushka in the sky.

>B. Imagine winning the lottery. Calculate what you would do for Tikkun Olam with a percentage of those millions of dollars.

Of course, if you are always on the look-out for Tzedakah opportunities, all of the above will come naturally to you. In retrospect, most likely #1-10 will seem like a very short list, and you will discover that you may not even need reminders at all.

How Can You "Get Better" at Giving Tzedakah?

Think of people who have just started out on a course of exercise and better eating habits to improve their health. They consult a nutritionist, hire a personal trainer, or talk to a friend who already has experience in the exercise room. Subsequently, they begin to eat better, trim their body fat, tone their bodies, and the "numbers" at the doctor's office stabilize nicely. (And, of course, they begin to *feel* better.)

The analogy holds for Tzedakah.

One part of "getting better at Tzedakah" is learning the basic Jewish texts, concepts, and principles involved. Just as people who are "cleaning up their act" physically need to know that "exercising three times a week for 30 minutes" produces such-and-such likely results, so, too, there are basic Jewish sources that serve as a guide to giving Tzedakah. Many of these sources appear throughout this book.

The other part is *doing* Tzedakah, giving your money away. The more you do it, the more you will get a clear sense of what is right or wrong, good or bad, more efficient or less efficient. Gauging your Tzedakah progress may be more difficult than measuring the results of your health regimen. In this quest, you can easily:

1. Count the pounds you have lost;

1. Compare 18-minute miles to 20-minute miles on your walks a month ago,

1. Read the various numbers from the lab work.

Charting your Tzedakah progress and rate-of-progress is not so straightforward. What criteria you choose for improving your Tzedakah giving will depend on your own sense of priorities combined with Jewish values. Some possibilities might include:

1. The *absolute* increase in dollars you donate;

1. The *percentage* increase of donations compared to your overall income;

1. How successful you have been at leveraging your Tzedakah money, i.e., how often did you get $200, $500, or $1,000 worth of Tikkun Olam from your $100 donation;

1. How many lives you may have changed for the better by your contributions;

1. How profoundly you may have changed the lives of others, whether a single person or many people;

1. How much more at ease you feel if you don't get special recognition or a thank-you,

1. Possibly how much less you feel resentment that you are giving away your "hard-earned" money. (You should be aware that many people who are *really* good at Tzedakah sometimes still feel a tinge of resentment.)

Some items in the 1-7 list may not apply to your giving. You may have others that are more relevant. However you determine your personal improvement, the more you *do* Tzedakah, the more you will develop the criteria best suited for measuring your own progress.

One final note: As I stated above, "getting better at Tzedakah" is part Torah study and part performing the actual Mitzvah of Tzedakah by giving. This is the final element in my analogy to exercise and diet. Just as you will get no benefit from learning all there is to know about diet and exercise unless you eat your apples and turn the TV on as you crank up the treadmill, so, too, all the knowledge and theory about Tzedakah you may acquire about Tzedakah is of little benefit unless you actually give away the Tzedakah money, and some person in need begins to live a better life. Torah study and doing Tzedakah are both crucial elements — but it is the actual *doing-the-Mitzvah* that will be the final proof of your progress.

How Do You Avoid
Making "Less-Than-Wise" Decisions
When You Are Giving Away
Your Tzedakah Money?

I have been thinking about this question for many years. I have reviewed it with dozens of friends and my personal Tzedakah teachers countless times. The following is the best analysis I can think of, to date.

The Tzedakah Disconnect: Analogies

Consider some of the recommendations in this guide about doing research about a particular Tzedakah program. Most of them are simple and logical. Now, think about the questions you ask when:

1. you need to purchase a car, a dining room table, or a stove, or

2. you are looking to hire someone to repair the roof or fix a leaky faucet, an electrician, or a babysitter, or

3. you are considering a job offer, or

4. you want to hire a partner for your business, or

5. the time has come for you to engage a perceptive attorney to help you write your will, or

6. sadly, you or some family member or friend has been diagnosed with a serious disease and you desperately need to begin your potentially life-and-death search for the right physician to manage the protocol.

You know what you need; you use various methods to get the proper information; you ask for advice from people who have done it before or otherwise are experts in the field, and, before you make your final decision, you weigh the various options in your mind.

Once all of the above is taken into account — then, *and only then*, do you commit.

The disconnect is that, when it comes to giving Tzedakah, sometimes some or all of these most elementary steps fall by the wayside.

One example — buying a computer — should make this clear. First, is the person selling you the Mac or PC primarily concerned with what your personal needs are? Second, has the salesperson covered everything? Do you do graphics? Compose music? Do slide shows or videos work for business presentations?...And if not, is he or she trying to sweet talk you and sell you a bill of goods loaded with things you don't need? Third, is the price — the cost to the dealer and the profit margin — reasonable? And, finally, will this G4 Powerbook laptop *really* do everything it is supposed to do, and will it do it with no unreasonable need for constant monitoring and repair? All of these questions analogize to where you are giving your Tzedakah money.

Furthermore, it may even be that sometime in the past you were "burned", as in:

1. the mattress you bought from a fast-talking salesperson was not the same one that was delivered, and the merchant refuses to exchange it, or

2. the money-back guarantee didn't apply to your purchase because of a technicality, or

3. you may have fallen for something "too good to be true" which, in fact, turned out to be too good to be true, or

4. when you were interviewing for a new job, the human services person swore up and down that your supervisor would work closely with you to teach you everything you needed to know, only to have him or her slough off the responsibility and leave you to muddle your way through the intricate tasks.

You learned very quickly, not only in your mind, but also in your gut, that *the next time* you will need to proceed more carefully, sometimes *much more* carefully.

Unfortunately, when it comes to Tzedakah, one additional element enters the picture. Again, for three decades I have had conversations on this topic, with people of all ages and economic status. All too frequently, I have found that many people more readily abandon Tzedakah altogether after being burned only once or twice. This is a serious problem and one that needs to be addressed by everyone concerned about Tikkun Olam.

Tzedakah Thinking

Speech, logic, and physical dexterity originate in distinct locations of the brain. The right half and left half of your brain produce different manifestations of your behavior. Research on both healthy and damaged or diseased brains reveal more answers to age-old mysteries than you could have imagined even 10 years ago. To a certain extent, genes, chemicals, electrical charges, and brain geography in isolation or in interconnection help explain who you are and how you function.

It may be that Tzedakah thinking involves a different part of the brain. It is possible that endorphins and other complex molecular structures are activated when you respond to the cry of a weeping child who has been abused. These same chemicals may be "taking a Shabbat nap" because they are not needed when you tell the mechanic that your car shimmies uncontrollably.

With all this talk about Tzedakah thinking, you are probably wondering, "Maybe there are people who are 'Tzedakah-challenged'?" Maybe there is some genetic deficiency or chemical imbalance in the "Tzedakah" area of the brain that would prevent them from doing this vital Mitzvah beautifully, or at all? You may justifiably wonder about that as you consider people who are doing very well and should know better than to keep it all to themselves. Even in those extreme cases, though, and you consider physiologically "Tzedakah-challenged" people, there are teachers who can work with them, just as special needs teachers can help students with dyslexia or dyscalculia.

I would suspect, though, that the issue is not essentially neurological in origin. If there are some people who have TzDS (Tzedakah Deficiency Syndrome), they are rare. There is no reason to assume that you, yourself, and most other people are anything other than medically well within the norm. I think the crux of the matter is this: You may have thought that Tzedakah comes naturally, and that it is something you just automatically know how to do. In my opinion, this is true only to a certain extent. Consider the following two points:

1. Becoming "good at Tzedakah" requires knowledge, training, and practice. Just as there are writing instructors who work with their students to help them write their best prose or poetry, so, too, you can find teachers and advisors who can work with your own talents and sensitivities and allow you to reach your maximum Tzedakah potential.

2. There are *some* people who seem to have "the natural touch" with Tzedakah and whose very essence is Tzedakah at its best. But even those people who *do* have the natural touch need to refine their skills. It is no different than a great opera singer who still needs a voice teacher or a home run slugger who works regularly with a batting coach.

Again, in my opinion, skill is skill and the analogies hold. But even if Mitzvah thinking is an altogether different skill, the significant odds are that you can master most, if not all, of it. With elementary or moderate guidance from the right teacher, you will become more proficient at Fixing the World with your Tzedakah money. The right teachers *do* exist, ones who understand not only the non-profit world and fundraising, but who also understand Tzedakah. They are not difficult to find, and once you begin to search for them, you may be surprised that so many of them exist or even that they exist at all. Remember, too, that they, themselves, have teachers and advisors (Tzedakah Rebbis) when they are confronted with difficult situations that are beyond their own expertise. *Everyone* needs to continue learning about Tzedakah.

Why Some People Give

You most likely want to give Tzedakah because you are concerned for the wellbeing of others. You sincerely want to do Tikkun Olam, to repair some aspect of what is bad, wrong, unjust, broken, or terribly messy in the vast array of things already in disarray or due to fall apart in the future — unless something serious and concrete is done *now*. The question then arises, "Why do some people who ostensibly share your point of view still manage to make less-than-wise decisions?"

I would begin to answer by suggesting that there are several other factors that affect some individuals' (and foundations') decisions, sometimes in a detrimental way. Among them are:

1. sentimental feelings,

2. a sudden influx of enormous income,

3. the occasion of honoring or memorializing a deceased parent or friend,

4. the need for attention because Mommy and Daddy never thought their child would amount to much in life,

5. a craving for flattery (whatever the psychological roots),

6. the need to repair a damaged reputation,

7. a desire for Kavod (being publicly honored),

8. the desire to keep up with the Cohens, Cohns, Kahns, Kahans, Cahans, or Kagans who are substantial givers,

9. the need to gain entrée into an exclusive circle within the community or to meet glitterati,

10. the need to build business connections,

11. the Tzedakah advisor had his or her own interests in mind rather than those of the donor and the recipients,

12. even a enthusiasm to do something good. This may turn into a hyper- or manic enthusiasm, which can cloud the donor's ability to "think" Tzedakah clearly.

All of these factors, alone or in various combinations, may possibly interfere with making sound Tzedakah decisions.

To illustrate — #2, "a sudden influx of enormous income". My long-time friend, Marc Pollick, established The Giving Back Fund because he saw a very real donor's need. He noticed that there were many stars, celebrities, and other high-profile people who needed to sharpen their Tzedakah skills and leverage their fame to bring about greater Tikkun Olam. The fund (**www.givingback.org**) has many programs, but I remember one particularly sensible example that Marc mentioned in one of our conversations. He explained: Take a young basketball star, maybe 21 years old and fresh out of college. He is getting a $7,000,000-a-year salary for five years, plus a $2,500,000 signing bonus. This young man, a caring person, wants to do something for his old neighborhood. It is sinking into greater physical disrepair, and the kids growing up there are sliding into a life of despair. He knows that a first-class basketball court and sports program will get many of these potentially dead-end kids off the streets and on to the right track. He knows that once he can get them to compete in a healthy manner, he can hope that his program will expand to after-school tutoring and other beneficial programs.

Here is where Giving Back steps in: A young man such as this one has no idea whatsoever *how* to get from Point A to Point B. How much should it *really* cost? How do you find the right person to make it a reality? How much should this person be paid? Marc explained that there are many people who already do this, but take an unreasonable, even outrageous, percentage of the Tzedakah money as their a fee. As a result, the basketball star's $500,000 becomes a mere $50,000 worth of benefit for the kids. Marc and Giving Back have changed all of that. His concern is to share the vision of the basketball star, to fine-tune the actual project, and to bring it to fruition for a cost befitting someone whose ultimate concern is First Class Tzedakah and Tikkun Olam with integrity.

...and Yet

Every day, well-intended, but misplaced, Tzedakah is happening. And it is being done by people with sums ranging from $1.00 to a gazillion dollars to donate to Tzedakah. And most of the donors are good-hearted, caring, and *well-meaning* people.

It is still being done every day, by people (most of them good-hearted, caring, *well-meaning* people), who, by doing so, may unwittingly be depriving more suitable Mitzvah heroes or organizations from receiving critically-needed Tzedakah money for their own Tikkun Olam work.

It is still being done every day by people — most of them good-hearted, caring, and well-meaning — but who *should* know better and *could* know better with just a little bit of effort on their part.

...and Yet

As this chapter, as well as others in this guide indicate, the situation *can* change.

What needs to be learned, can be partially learned alone, and the rest studied with the appropriate Tzedakah advisor. This advisor can provide direction that builds on a combination of the giver's own personality and wishes and the needs that most demand attention.

Doing Tzedakah better is *not* the same as asking people whose organic learning disability prevents them from doing better in math at school. Nor is it analogous to asking the most uncoordinated people to train for an Olympic gymnastics event. The skills, techniques, and ability to ask the right questions needed to do Tzedakah better are neither arcane nor hocus-pocus. Look around you, activate *every* part of your brain, and you will know which questions to ask.

As stated above, the material to be learned is all "learnable", no matter where your starting point may be.

In Conclusion, Back to the Jewish Sources

The words of Deuteronomy 30:11-14, which refers to God's teaching in general, would certainly apply to Tzedakah:

לא–נפלאת הוא ממך ולא–רחקה הוא
לא בשמים הוא
לאמר מי יעלה–לנו השמימה ויקחה לנו
וישמענו אתה ונעשנה
ולא–מעבר לים הוא
לאמר מי יעבר–לנו אל–עבר הים
ויקחה לנו וישמענו אתה ונעשנה
כי–קרוב אליך הדבר מאד
בפיך ובלבבך לעשתו

I paraphrase and interpret the translation:

...it is not so awesome that you cannot grasp it, nor overwhelmingly far away from you.
It is not in the Heavens that you should say,
"Who can go up there, bring it down, and explain it to us so we can do it."
It is not beyond the sea that you should say,
"Who will cross this vast expanse, get it, and explain it to us so we can do it. "
Eve- so-much to the contrary — it is incredibly close to you, already in your mouth when you express your desire to do Tzedakah and in your good and generous being to do."

7 Questions Concerning Using Your Money for Tzedakah

Complete the following:

1. *Have you used the same amount of brain-and-heart power to make decisions about your Tzedakah money as you did when you planned your personal budget? Circle one:*

YES   **NO**

If so, list some examples:

_____

_____

_____

2. *Have you studied the distinctly Jewish methods of giving Tzedakah and how they contrast with and compare to methods of giving in other religions and cultures? Circle one:*

YES   **NO**

If so, list things you learned from your study:

_____

_____

_____

3. *Are your Tzedakah advisors as skilled and wise about where to give Tzedakah as your accountant, stockbroker, insurance person, and other financial advisors? Circle one:*

YES   **NO**

If yes, list your Tzedakah advisors and what impresses you about their advice?

_____

_____

_____

4. Did you take into account that Tzedakah money often has more "buying power" than "regular money", i.e., that you can often change and save lives with less money than it takes to change the oil in your car? Circle one:

YES   NO

If so, give examples of "Tzedakah buying power" that particularly impressed you:

_____

_____

_____

5. Did you ever look at coins and dollar bills and think that — if properly donated — these ostensibly small sums of money could radically improve the lives of others?

YES   NO

If so, give examples.

_____

_____

_____

6. If you have looked at coins and dollar bills this way — did you ever think that you would be getting such enjoyment-☺☺☺☺ from giving your money away?

YES   NO

If so, what words would you use to explain this unique feeling to others?

_____

_____

_____

7 Did you ever imagine that, once you began to do Tikkun Olam to this extent — changing and saving lives with money — that you would want to do more and more of it, even if it meant that you might have less money for your personal use?

YES   NO

Now, review your answers and write a paragraph articulating how you would describe your relationship to both kinds of money — money for your own use and Tzedakah money.

_____

_____

_____

_____

_____

_____

_____

_____

_____

_____

_____

_____

_____

_____

When Is a "Good Time" to Give Tzedakah?

Regularly: 1) hourly, (2) daily, (3) weekly, (4) monthly, or any combination of 1-4, or all of them

Before lighting the candles for Shabbat and holidays

Long enough before Shabbat or holidays to make certain others have been provided for so that they, too, can also enjoy Shabbat or the holiday

When you arrive in Israel and throughout your time in Israel

On יום העצמאות-Yom HaAtzma'ut, Israel Independence Day (the 5th of the Hebrew month of Iyyar)

On יום הזכרון-Yom Hazikaron, The Day of Remembrance for fallen Israeli soldiers (the 4th of Iyyar)

On יום ירושלים-Yom Yerushalayim The Anniversary of the Reunification of Jerusalem, June 1967 (the 28th of Iyyar)

On יום הזכרון לשואה ולגבורה-Yom HaZikaron LaShoah VeLaGevura, Remembrance Day for Victims of the Shoah-Holocaust, and Resistance During the Shoah (the 27th of Nissan)

Whenever you feel like it

Whenever you don't feel like it, but you know that it is a Mitzvah

Whenever you don't feel like it, but you have learned about a serious need

Whenever you feel particularly happy

Whenever you feel particularly sad, down, lonely, or depressed

When you have made a serious promise that if X happens, you will donate Y dollars to Tzedakah. In the classic Jewish legal sense of the term, a "נדר-neder, vow" is a *formal* verbal declaration. Jewish texts as far back as Biblical times describe the proper procedures for fulfilling the vow. At certain times in your life, you may make an "If this…, then this…" kind of promise in a most serious frame of mind. While this may not be exactly the same as a neder-vow, your intense sincerity was and is of great importance to you. Completing the process, i.e., donating to Tzedakah, can be a very fulfilling Life-experience.

During a week-day Minyan

On the occasion of a Brit Milah (Bris), baby naming, Bar or Bat Mitzvah, Wedding, and other Jewish or secular joyous life-cycle event — *anyone's*

When you or someone else — God forbid — is hospitalized, has a serious illness, or has received word of a troubling medical diagnosis

When you or someone else has recovered from illness

On a relative's or friend's yahrtzeit

When you learn that a friend's relative has died

On the occasion of a friend's becoming a Jew-by-choice

Birthdays and anniversaries – *anyone's*

When you hang a Mezuzzah on the doorposts of your house or apartment

When you get a gift of money, receive a grant, or inherit money

When you purchase something for yourself that will bring you happiness or comfort, or will serve as a useful tool or instrument either for your work or for your Tikkun Olam work

When you purchase a knickknack or *tchatchka* that is just for fun or just because you like it, or it fulfills your childhood fantasies — even if it looks weird or ruins the aesthetics of your kitchen or living room

When you get hired for the job you always wanted

When you get a promotion or a raise or both

When you get fired from your job, and you are so happy because you hated your boss and the working conditions, and this is exactly what you needed to strike out on your own

Whenever you don't feel any specific high or low moment in your life

Whenever you feel things have become too humdrum and routine

Whenever you need to or *really* need to — for your own personal reasons

When your child, nephew, niece, granddaughter, grandson or friend's child, nephew, niece, grandchild is born

When your child takes his or her first steps

When your child goes for his or her first day to school

When your child gets a good report card

When your child does not get a good report card, but you stop for a moment and consider how much you love your child just because she or he is *your* child. You remind yourself that good grades are not as important as loving and caring for each other. Then you look your child in the eye and tell your child exactly that — how much you love her or him just because she or he is your daughter or son, no matter what grades he or she gets in school. And even if you *know* that he or she could have "tried harder".

When your child gets his or her driver's license and does his or her first Mitzvah using the car as a *Mitzvah* vehicle

When your child gets into her or his first choice for college

When your child doesn't get into her or his first choice for college but says, "Abba, Eema, it's OK, there are more important things in life."

When you are helping your child pack for college and you hand her or him a Tzedakah box to put in the suitcase

At tax time, when you review the need for more tax deductions

At tax time, without any concern for the need for more tax deductions

For no particular reason at all

For good reason, but none that you can *consciously* think of

All the time

Whenever…

How Much Are You Supposed to Give?

שיעור נתינתה: אם ידו משגת יתן כפי צורך העניים
ואם אין ידו משגת כל כך
יתן עד חומש נכסיו מצוה מן המובחר
ואחד מעשרה מדה בינונית פחות מכאן עין רעה...
הגה ואל יבזבז אדם יותר מחומש שלא יצטרך לבריות

The amount one should give to Tzedakah:
If one can afford it, enough to respond to all of the needs of the poor people.
But if one cannot afford that much,
then one should give up to a fifth of one's possessions —
which is doing the Mitzvah in an exceptional fashion —
one tenth is an average percentage,
and less is considered "poor eyesight" [i.e., giving less than needed because
you may not have recognized how great the needs are]....
and one should not give away more than 20%,
lest he or she ultimately becomes dependent on others.

Shulchan Aruch, Yoreh De'ah 249:1

It <u>Is</u> All Right to Be Wealthy

Judaism does not set an upper limit to how much money a person should have. There is no prohibition against being wealthy. Certainly our tradition speaks out against people who are overly self-indulgent, but — *in and of itself* — there is nothing wrong with being a Rothschild, or one, two, or ten levels below "Rothschildkeit." As mentioned elsewhere in this book, the Jewish justification was expressed by someone whose father had said, "If you are going to *live* large, *give* large." In fact, in the practical world of fundraising, the different levels of wealth come into serious play. A mere millionaire may not be able to sway a multi-millionaire to give to a worthy Tzedakah project. Often, only a multi-millionaire soliciting another multi-millionaire can do it. "Big Money" works differently than "Small Money" in the Tzedakah sphere, just as it does in the "regular world". For example, to purchase and build a new Jewish camp such as Ramah Darom, the founders needed a large base of Big Tzedakah Money. Nickels and dimes usually aren't capable of doing that type of Tikkun Olam. On several occasions, smaller donations multiplied by the thousands or millions *have* created the giant programs, but the general rule is you have to start with guarantees of hundreds of thousands or millions of dollars.

Consider big and small money in daily life: If you are buying a house, you won't usually quibble over $100 here or there. On the other hand, if you are in the supermarket and you notice that the price of Anjou pears has jumped 50¢ a pound in the last week, you may not buy them. So, too with Tzedakah money: For some people, it's all the same whether they give $2 million or $3 million for a worthy Tikkun Olam program. For others, the quarter they donate on a given occasion according to that moment's available Tzedakah money is equally defined as "Tzedakah". Both the huge sums and the (mis-labeled) "small" money make a difference.

It Is _Not_ All Right to Impoverish Yourself Doing Tzedakah

Throughout the discussion in the previous two paragraphs, it should be clear that there is no Jewish ideal of self-impoverishment. Giving away all of your money and your possessions to do Tzedakah for others is _not_ Jewish. In fact, in his classic Mishnah Torah law code, Maimonides states it with these stark words:

...ואין זו חסידות אלא שטות
שהרי הוא מאבד כל ממונו ויצטרך לבריות...
ובזה וכיוצא בו אמרו חכמים חסיד שוטה מכלל מבלי עולם

...this is not righteousness, but rather foolishness. Giving away all one's money causes that person to be in need of others....this is one of the situations the sages referred to when they taught, "A foolish righteous person is among those who 'wear the world out.'"

Hilchot Arachin Va'Charamin 8:13

By "wear the world out", Maimonides means — that person becomes an additional drain on available resources. This is a setback to Tikkun Olam, not a step forward. And that is why the rule is "One should not give away more than 20%".

Fixing EverythingThat Is Wrong in the Entire World

Now for the hard part — the opening lines of the Jewish law states:

The amount one should give to Tzedakah:
If one can afford it, enough to answer all the needs of the poor people.
But if one cannot afford that much, then…

Two comments:

1. This Jewish law can be traced back to Talmudic times, with sources going even further back to the Torah. In the Biblical and Talmudic mind, "all the needs of the poor people" meant a considerably smaller frame of reference than in today's world: your neighborhood, your village, your town, possibly your small city. It would be inconceivable to even the greatest Tzaddik in the Bible or Talmud that people could be connected by such technology as simple (to us in the 21st century) as a telephone, let alone a fax machine, radio, TV, and now e-mail and the internet. For us, "next door" is absolutely anywhere in the world. No one person could possibly satisfy "all the needs of the poor people" today. And yet —

2. The opening line of the הלכה-Halachah, Jewish law remains valid. On first reading, you might react and say that this kind of thinking might be psychologically crushing. You do your part in Tikkun Olam, and yet, you always know that there is a Big Wide World of other needs out there

left to be done. You might become paralyzed by a feeling of guilt, inadequacy, or even utter helplessness, or you might increase your activities to the point of burn-out.

I understand the opening statement differently. I think what the Shulchan Aruch (and the Bible and Talmud before that) is teaching us is that *total* Tikkun Olam is *ultimately* doable. There exists an incredible sum-total of needs; I don't dispute that fact. But, combined with working for systemic change, each person doing individual, personalized Tzedakah joins every other person doing the same. This yields a similarly huge sum-total of Tikkun Olam. The outcome *can* be a world-in-repair. When considered in this light, the opening lines of the text — "Enough to respond to all of the needs of the poor people" — express an extremely *positive* approach to Tzedakah. I believe that they are an optimistic, energizing force for all who would wish to make the world a better, more Menschlich place *for everyone*.

The Jewish Percentage and Procedure

Basing his ruling on Biblical text (Leviticus 27:28) and centuries-old traditions, Maimonides states that 10-20% is the appropriate amount to give to Tzedakah. Several comments will expand on his ruling:

1. According to most Jewish legal authorities, these percentages are to be calculated *after* taxes.

2 There *are* a few exceptions to the 20% upper limit, among them:

> A. If you are wealthy and there is no danger of your becoming dependent on others to meet your basic needs.

> B. You are permitted to give away more than 20% in a last will and testament.

> C. Securing the release of people in captivity. The assumption is that they are always in imminent danger of being killed. Sadly, the numerous savage murders of hostages in the Iraq War prove this point.

Reviewing the paragraphs above, it is clear that Jewish tradition affords you a range of possibilities. Within the specific range of percentages, you are afforded a certain flexibility and latitude to express your individualism and creativity.

One final comment to those who claim that they are neither creative nor talented: You may consider yourself a failure at piano or pottery-making, tone-deaf or athletically unfit for any sport other than checkers. Nevertheless, I assure you that there is every reason to believe that you will find yourself capable of true excellence, incredible creativity, and great distinction in your Tzedakah efforts.

What Can You Do If Your Money Is Limited?

Your personal financial situation may range from being nearly-Bill-Gates-rich, to very comfortable, to modest, to "just getting by". Even if you are doing well, there may be things that happen that cause your actual money to shrink to levels which may cause you to think, "I need to cut back on my Tzedakah giving." That may be a natural tendency, but three Jewish texts address this issue and offer important insights for limited-income or fixed-income individuals, couples, and families.

Giving Money Away Incurs No Personal Loss

לעולם אין אדם מעני מן הצדקה

ואין דבר רע ולא היזק נגלל בשביל הצדקה

שנאמר והיה מעשה הצדקה שלום

No one ever becomes poor from doing Tzedakah,

nor does anything bad/horrible/unpleasant nor damaging result from
Tzedakah,

as the verse states,

"and the end result of Tzedakah will be שלום-Shalom."

Maimonides, Mishnah Torah,
Matnot Ani'im, Laws of Gifts to Poor People, 10:2,
Isaiah 32:17

At first glance, this text sounds merely like a nice, comforting theme for a sermon. The Rabbis, however, were very practical-minded people, and they meant the words to be taken more seriously than simple sermonics. They had a deep understanding of day-to-day human existence.

The rabbis were anything but naïve. They were constantly and *passionately* discussing why bad things happen to good people. I don't know just how much they believed a generous person's Tzedakah may protect them from the venom of a snakebite, but they clearly understood that Tikkun Olam people would be protected from other potentially lethal forms of injury. They believed that Tzedakah could diminish the damaging force of insecurity, fear, and anxiety. That is why they used the term "דבר רע-davar ra". "רע-ra" has a range of meaning which includes everything from "not good" to "toxic" to "lethal" to "catastrophic".

Another text, mentioned earlier in this guide (Jerusalem Talmud [Venice Edition], Terumot 8:10) focuses specifically on the realities of money and how much it affects daily life:

כל האיברים תלויין בלב והלב תלוי בכיס

Every part of the human body depends on the heart,
But the heart depends on the pocket.

In the quote from Maimonides' stated above, the intent is that giving Tzedakah "enriches" your life, and that, if you are a giver, you will always feel at home in Life. You will never be impoverished by loneliness or fear of abandonment…because you are *always* connected to other people because of your acts of Tzedakah. Therefore, on an even more practical level, Maimonides and the Talmudic Rabbis also meant that giving your Tzedakah money strengthens your local, even global, society, people function better, the social order works more smoothly, and, as a result, you would not need to spend as much of your own money to live your own life as "normally" as before. You have made the world better, and while this is philosophically invaluable, in real dollars and cents, it means day-to-day living costs less.

To illustrate: Suppose you donate to a scholarship fund for at-risk kids. As a result, six more potentially dysfunctional children whose needs would have cost a fortune for therapy and care will (1) continue their education, (2) go to summer camp, (3) get into a job training program, and (4) become accomplished business people (hi-tech/physicians/chefs). They, in turn, donate their portion of Tzedakah back into the Great Pool of Tzedakah money, and everyone benefits.

Another illustration: Suppose you contribute some of your Tzedakah money to Independent Transportation Network (ITN) founded by Kathy Freund in Portland, Maine. Originally established in her local community, it continues to expand to many other cities in the United States. (**www.itnamerica.org**) ITN provides a heavily-discounted, *personal* transportation service for individuals no longer able to drive. Your elderly aunt and uncle no longer drive, cannot take public transportation for a variety of reasons, and do not have enough money for cab fares for their normal needs. Perhaps you used to send them $100 a month to help out. Now, you don't have to subsidize this particular need, because of Kathy's transportation network. Multiply that system of interconnections by thousands of other possibilities. Now Maimonides' and the Rabbis' statements make much more *practical* sense.

Why Poor People are Expected to Give Tzedakah

אמר מר זוטרא אפילו עני המתפרנס מן הצדקה יעשה צדקה

Mar Zutra said:
Even a poor person who is supported by Tzedakah must give Tzedakah.

Gittin 7b

There are many reasons why Judaism expects poor people to give. The "high" reason is that if you take away a person's self-definition as a giver, you have taken away his or her self-dignity. This is an incredibly serious offense. As I have noted, my teacher, Rabbi Bradley Shavit Artson, says it beautifully, "Tzedakah is not about giving; Tzedakah is about being." Being a Tzedakah-giver defines *who you are* as a person and as a Jew. To tell anyone that she or he is too poor to give is, in a way, tantamount to taking away her or his very existence.

Other reasons why poor people have to give include: (1) the poor person's actual dollars are *needed* in the overall pool of available Tzedakah funds, (2) the poor person knows how hard it is to live in serious financial difficulty and, therefore, may know better where to give Tzedakah money, and (3) with more money in the general pool available, better services will be provided by Mitzvah heroes and their Tikkun Olam programs to improve the poor person's life.

Not Poor, But Not Wealthy or Even "Comfortable"

דרש רב עוירא זימנין א"ל משמיה דרב אמי
וזמנין אמר לה משמיה דרב אסי...
אם רואה אדם שמזונותיו מצומצמין
יעשה מהן צדקה וכ"ש כשהן מרובין

Rabbi Avira taught —
sometimes in the name of Rabbi Ammi
and sometimes in the name of Rabbi Assi:...
If a person sees that his or her [financial] resources are limited,
he or she should use them for Tzedakah,
and so much the more so when he or she has great [financial] resources.

Gittin 7a

Reasons for giving when your income is limited are similar to those listed in the previous section, with, perhaps, one important addition: The idea of "limited income" may vary much more in *your* mind than what it means to *actually* be poor. "Limited income" calls for an examination and re-examination of what you consider necessities for living a decent life, and what are only luxuries you can live without.

Rich, comfortable, living on a tight budget, or just "getting by", studies show that, while there may be trends, there is no absolute pattern to giving. Statistics often show that, in general, people in lower income brackets are better givers, but, with or without statistics and studies, your concern is your own pattern and extent of giving. While there certainly are generous wealthy and super-wealthy people, there are, as well, some very wealthy individuals who are not particularly philanthropic. There are also people with limited income who are penny-pinchers, and still others who give with a hand always open to others. *Every* type of giver or non-giver exists in *every* income bracket. As stated above, though, your personal concern is *your own giving*. You will evaluate what you have, what you don't have, what you need, what you don't really need, and what others need, and then you will decide — with guidance from Jewish thought and practice — where to give accordingly.

What Is a Tzedakah Program's "Wish List", and Why Is It Sometimes Especially Important to Get a "Wish List" Before You Donate?

By Way of Introduction, Two Kinds of Wish Lists

In actuality there are two kinds of wish lists. One is a catalogue of *actual* needs, and the other is a list of needs plus an "add-on". By an "add-on", I mean, the amount you would contribute for the "Kavod", the honor of being recognized publicly for your donation. This includes items such as having the reading room in a library named for you. The *actual* cost may be $200,000, but your expected donation is $500,000, because the room will always be known as the Porath Reading Room. This chapter deals with only the former type of wish list, namely, actual costs of the item.

Why There Are Wish Lists

No matter how recently a brochure, annual report, or website has been updated, there are often many late-breaking needs for any Mitzvah hero or Tzedakah organization. Time and again, needs arise even a few hours before you contact the Mitzvah hero or organization. The "wish list" focuses on *what is needed right at that moment*. Usually, the wish list is a catalogue of short-term needs, including items that may be immediately solvable by your personal donation. To name a few: The delivery truck for a food recycling operation may desperately need new tires or insurance *now*, a shelter for victims of domestic violence may need to pay rent and utilities *now*, the price of gasoline has risen and operations are grinding to a halt because the Mitzvah hero can no longer afford to reach all of the people with whom she or he is working to restore them to good physical or mental health.

There are even situations where long-term needs have become a higher priority on the wish list. After months of discussion, you may be in touch just at the time when a Mitzvah hero or organization has decided to develop a new program because the demand for that kind of Tikkun Olam has become so great. Of infinite possibilities, the following three examples should illustrate my point:

1. Someone appears as if "out of nowhere" who could be an ideal year-long assistant to help expand the program.

2. After a natural disaster, a dozen families that previously had manageable needs, now have to re-locate and begin a new life. They have been left with nothing but the clothing they wore when they were rescued. The demands for Tzedakah money may be enormous.

3. A recent wave of immigrants from Ethiopia has just arrived in Israel, and accommodating for their needs has placed greater demands on the organization

that is working with them. Depending on the circumstances, the wish list for both short-term and long-term needs can be *very* long.

Why You Might Ask to See a Wish List

In addition, your personal reasons for asking for the wish list may include:

1. The Mitzvah hero's or organization's work is so extensive, you would like to focus on a specific aspect of the Tikkun Olam work so that your donation will not be "swallowed up" in the overall program.

2. You like to feel that you have *totally* eliminated at least one of the Mitzvah heroes' or organizations' needs. (They like to hear words like, "I can do that" or "Solved! Next...")

3. You want to have as great an impact on their Tikkun Olam work as possible.

The following suggestions may be of use as you do your research on this aspect of your Tzedakah work:

1. Once you have located Mitzvah heroes or Tikkun Olam programs that appeal to you, contact them directly.

2. Make certain to speak to the person who is most knowledgeable about the *real* needs and who is best able to tell you all the details.

3. Ask if your donation is needed more for discretionary use, for wish list items, or a combination of both.

4. If the person says that wish list items are critical, give him or her a general range of how much Tzedakah money you are considering donating to the Tikkun Olam work. Even if you are thinking of giving "only" $18 or $25, there is no need to be embarrassed. You have been open with them, and you may find something on a wish list that fits your Tzedakah giving so well, you will decide to donate more than you had originally intended. This happens frequently with wish lists.

5. If something on the wish list particularly appeals to you, you may want to divide your contribution so that a portion helps to cover their overall work *and* another portion is dedicated to something on the wish list.

6. You will often discover that you are so taken by the wish list, you may decide to contribute 100% of what you had already decided to donate *plus* additional Tzedakah money for the items on the wish list. This, too, happens frequently.

A concluding thought: Working with wish lists may well fit your own pattern of Tzedakah. After more than 30 years of experience with my own Ziv Tzedakah Fund, I have found that this aspect of giving makes a *huge* difference and is worth your serious consideration.

How Can You Make the Most of Your Tzedakah Money?

"Bang for the Buck" in Regular Life

In "regular" life you stretch your money all the time:

You look for department store sales.

You compare prices before buying insurance, a computer, or a car.

You have finally reached the age when you get senior citizen discounts at the movies and on trains and planes.

You use coupons from newspapers, magazines, and flyers that come in the mail.

You love "twofers" — two tickets to a play for the price of one.

You surf the internet for the lowest possible airfares.

Colloquially, you call this "getting more bang for the buck", and rarely would you opt for a higher price if you could stretch your money by any reasonable means.

"Bang for the Tzedakah Buck"

You can stretch your Tzedakah money to accomplish more Tikkun Olam, Just as you do in "regular" life. In most cases this is known as "leveraging your Tzedakah money". Here are just a few examples:

1. **Interest-free loan societies:** A particularly beautiful way to leverage your Tzedakah money is to support a Jewish interest-free loan society. In Hebrew it is called a גמ"ח-Gemach, an abbreviation for "גמילות חסד-Gemillut Chessed", an act of caring lovingkindness. The Jewish practice of offering interest-free loans extends back millennia to Biblical times. The beauty of it is that the money continues to re-circulate. Once loans begin to be repaid, that money goes right back out for other loans. And most Gemachs have a default rate of less than three or four percent. To give you a sense of the "rate of return" on an interest-free loan investment, Ziv Tzedakah Fund's cumulative donations to the Israel Free Loan Association over approximately 15 years totaled $51,484. As of April, 2006, this sum had generated $284,040 in the form of 237 loans — a return of 552%! Surf the website of the International Association of Hebrew Free Loans (IAHFL) at **www.freeloan.org** to learn more about interest-free loans.

2. **Matching Funds:** *Once you have found Mitzvah heroes or Tzedakah programs you want to support,* you may find that they have been offered a matching grant. Every dollar you give will be matched one-for-one, two-for-one, or even more by some other donor. A striking example is this: In the aftermath of the devastation of

Hurricane Katrina, one individual lined up several people who committed to match donations. By the time he had finished creating his Tzedakah-consortium, he had assembled an eight-to-one arrangement. This meant that for every $100 you donated, it actually amounted to $900 for Katrina relief.

3. *Their* **expertise:** Through your research, you may discover Mitzvah heroes who are experts at obtaining discounts for goods and services they need in their Mitzvah work. Because what they are doing is *so* right and *so* good, others may want to join them by offering everything at cost or for free. Your Mitzvah money will stretch nicely if you know that a Mitzvah hero who needs to buy a van has done *her or his* research and can purchase it at cost.

4. **Built into the Mitzvah hero's project:** Similarly, if a Mitzvah hero retrieves food from hotels, restaurants, and other food establishments and provides the food for people in need, your donation of $100 may equal as much as, or more than, 10 times the store-purchased value. For instance, you may decide to pay $300 to rent a bus to bring volunteers to an orchard to glean the fruit. A day's gleaning could easily yield $5,000-$10,000 worth of clementines, onions, or strawberries for food banks and soup kitchens.

5. **Mitzvah hero partnerships:** You may also find a Mitzvah hero such as Joseph Gitler and his Table to Table program in Israel. (www.tabletotable.org.il) He is a supreme expert at "partnering" — working with already-established programs. He finds trustworthy local programs that provide food to people in need. His part, then, in providing for hungry people is simply to retrieve the food and get it from Point Alef to Point Bet, as with the fruit gleaning mentioned in #4. This saves tremendously on overhead costs. (In the United States, Ken Horne's Society of St. Andrew/The Potato Project is doing similarly astonishing work. **www.endhunger.org**)

6. **Your own initiative**: This, too, could play a vital role in stretching your Tzedakah money. For example, winter is about to hit your hometown of Minneapolis. You take it upon yourself to approach the owner or manager of a large clothing store and to say that you would like to buy sweaters for people in need. It *may* happen that the owner or manager will give you a discount, donate the sweaters, or give you both the discount and also add several sweaters (*and* sweatshirts, gloves, hats, and long underwear) as a donation from the store. Frequently, owners and managers can't help in this way because of too many similar requests, a slowdown in the economy, or similar reasons, but you should always feel that *you are entitled to ask.* It isn't necessary that you have a personal connection to the store, e.g., the owner is your old sorority sister from college. Because you are on a Mitzvah mission, you may feel moved to just do it "cold", and since you are not asking for yourself, you will almost always get a sympathetic response whether or not you actually get a discount or 100% donated items.

7. **At work:** Many corporate holiday parties have been cancelled or seriously downgraded to a less elaborate bash because *one individual* suggested it to the boss. (*You* could be that individual.) The money saved is then donated to an appropriate Tikkun Olam project. And more — many employees may feel moved to donate to the designated program, and your own donation will now represent substantially more dollar-benefit to the recipients.

8. **Testimonial dinners:** You may suggest to an organization that it change its annual dinner to a dessert reception. While it is true that these gatherings

powerfully publicize the good work, and the "electricity" in the room reinforces the attendees' commitment, many groups could accomplish the same with a dessert reception. The evening's expense will be greatly reduced, and a greater percentage of what everyone pays to attend the event will then go to the Tzedakah program's real work — doing Tikkun Olam.

Ray Buchanan's Incredible Feat of Leveraging

The best example of Tzedakah leveraging I learned of recently comes from Ray Buchanan, founder of Stop Hunger Now (SHN, **www.stophungernow.org**), an international relief organization providing food, medicines, and other critical items in several countries throughout the world. I have known Ray for many years, and Stop Hunger Now is always my first choice whenever a Tikkun Olam situation arises that falls within his realm of expertise. Responding to a question about an astonishing leveraging effort he made, this is what he reported:

Earlier this year, SHN was offered $18,000,000 of food if we could take care of all the shipping, transportation and admin costs...which amounted to $75,000. Almost at the same time, we were given the opportunity to provide $650,000 worth of critically needed medicines for Northern Uganda and Southern Sudan...if we could cover a $12,000 distribution cost.

We were able to do both...because of the generosity and faithfulness of our friends and supporters. **Working together allowed us to leverage $87,000 into almost $19,000,000 worth of life-saving food and medicine.**

By simple division, Buchanan's leveraging yields a return of more than $214 in delivered Mitzvah goods for every $1 contributed to Stop Hunger Now. This is truly a staggering accomplishment, and while few Mitzvah heroes and Tzedakah programs can achieve this exceptional degree of successful leveraging and partnering, the principle remains the same: By using your researching talents and common sense, your Tzedakah *can* often make things happen far beyond your imagining.

The "and Yet"

And yet, all the good intentions, exquisite sensitivity and desire to do good, and the massive sympathy of others would not have been enough if Ray did not have the actual $87,000 of Tzedakah he needed when he set out to provide so much good for so many people. When I teach, I usually tell my students, "You can't do $10 worth of Tikkun Olam with only $9 in Tzedakah money, or $100 worth of Tikkun Olam with only $90, or $1,000 worth with only $900." Buchanan, and others teach us that you can, indeed, do millions of dollars worth of Tikkun Olam with thousands of dollars. Now I add, "But you still need the thousands of dollars."

Why Does It Sometimes Feel So Difficult to Give Your Money Away?

אשרי משכיל אל דל

Happy is the person who is משכיל-Maskil in relation to the person in need.

Psalm 41:2

אמר ר' יונה אשרי נותן אל דל אין כת' כן
אלא אשרי משכיל אל דל הוי מסתכל בו היאך לזכות בו

Rabbi Yonah said,

"Happy is the person who <u>gives</u> to the person in need"

is not what the verse says, but rather,

"Happy is the one who is משכיל-Maskil in relation to the person in need,"

meaning,

"Look at the situation carefully,

and keep in mind how it is a <u>privilege</u> to do the Mitzvah through that person."

Leviticus Rabba 34:1; Margoliot Edition 4:773

Judaism considers giving Tzedakah a *privilege*. In the above passage, Rabbi Yonah wonders why Psalm 41 didn't use the verb "נתן-give". Why doesn't the verse simply state, "Happy is the person who *gives to* the person in need"? Instead, the word is "משכיל-Maskil", from the root "שכל". This is the same root in modern Hebrew and traditional Yiddish that gives us *Sechel*, usually translated as "common sense". Centuries ago, though, it meant the entire range of your mental, spiritual, psychological, and emotional capabilities, including your intelligence, imagination, talents, *and* common sense. Rabbi Yonah stresses that all of these aspects of your personality should come into play when you create a relationship with a person in need with your Tzedakah money.

What is particularly interesting are the Rabbi's closing words, "היאך לזכות בו". "לזכות-Lizkot", comes from the same Hebrew root as "זכות-privilege". Indeed, in that same chapter of the Midrash, a poor person says, "זכי בי-Zaki Bi–Have the privilege of doing Tzedakah through me." Once again, the same Hebrew root is used. In the language of the Jews nearly 2,000 years ago, this was a natural way to say, "I need help, and I have chosen *you* to be the one to set things right."

It may not be easy to shift your Mitzvahs, Tzedakah, and Tikkun Olam mindset to one of "privilege". Nevertheless, those who have succeeded in making the transition have told me that it feels as though a great weight has been lifted from their shoulders. Some have even described this insight as "revelatory", and that, as a result, their labors on behalf of others now give greater meaning to their lives.

How Important Is Your Attitude and Intent?

פחות מזה שיתן לו בעצב

A still lower level is giving בעצב-BeEtzev.

Maimonides, Mishnah Torah,
Hilchot Matnot Ani'im, Laws of Gifts to Poor People, 10:14

This is the 8th, the lowest, level in Maimonides' famous list of Tzedakah giving. The key word here is "בעצב". The root "עצב" can have many meanings including "sadness", "distress", "pain", and "labor" (including "labor pains"). The 8th level, therefore, means that the person is giving, but reluctantly, and is at great pains to donate. What is crucial to understand is that, even though giving grudgingly is at the bottom of the list, *it is still an act of Tzedakah*. **I cannot stress this point strongly enough.** The Jewish definition of Tzedakah is that you have taken some of your money and used it for the benefit of others. While it would be wonderful if everyone gave willingly and cheerfully, very *real* money is what is needed in the very *real* world of Tikkun Olam.

This text supports my position on public school community service requirements. In most high schools in the United States and *all* high schools in Israel, students are required to do a certain number of hours of community service in order to graduate. I think that this is one of the greatest ventures in the field of education...even if we arbitrarily estimate that 16% of the students do it only because it will look good on their college applications. I have no problem with that. Just consider the staggering number of lives that have been changed for the better since the service requirement was instituted in high schools. Give it a *real* number — say 100,000,000 lives. (I personally believe that that is a very conservative estimate.) If my Mitzvah math is correct that 16% of the students do their Tikkun Olam for less-than-100% pure goodness, then this means that 16,000,000 people are living better as a result of the students' community service requirement. Breaking the accepted rules of fine writing, I state again, "16,000,000 people are living better as a result of the students' community service requirement!!!!!!"

I rest my case.

Should You Always Do Your Tzedakah Giving Anonymously?

Background: Maimonides' Principles of Tzedakah and the Issue of Secret and Anonymous Giving

מעלה גדולה שאין למעלה ממנה זה המחזיק ביד ישראל שמך
ונותן לו מתנה או הלואה או עושה עמו שותפות או ממציא לו מלאכה
כדי לחזק את ידו עד שלא יצטרך לבריות לשאול...
פחות מזה הנותן צדקה לעניים ולא ידע למי נתן ולא ידע העני ממי לקח
שהרי זו מצוה לשמה...

The highest degree [of Tzedakah] is to strengthen the hand of a Jew who is poor, giving that person a gift, or a loan, or becoming a partner, or finding a job for that person — to strengthen the person's hand, so that the person can become self-supporting and will not have to be dependent on others....

One degree lower is a person who gives Tzedakah to poor people and is unaware of the recipient, who in turn is unaware of the giver. This is indeed a religious act achieved for its own sake....

Maimonides, Mishnah Torah,
Hilchot Matnot Ani'im, Laws of Gifts to Poor People, 10:7-8

At my lectures, I frequently ask, "What is Maimonides' *highest* level of Tzedakah?" Quite often the answer given is, "When the recipient doesn't know the donor, and when the donor doesn't know the recipient." Reading the actual source, though, we see that they are really responding to Maimonides' *second* level. The highest level includes finding someone a job so she or he can become self-sufficient. In that situation, you have to know enough about the person, perhaps even conducting an interview, in order to provide the appropriate match for employment.

Three additional examples provide a broader understanding of Maimonides' highest level of Tzedakah. Each requires "non-anonymity". (However, your donation to these kinds of Tzedakah organizations preserves your own anonymous relationship to the actual recipient.)

1. Pa'amonim-פעמונים is an organization in Israel that works specifically with a certain well-defined category of people who have fallen between the cracks of the government social service system. They are individuals and families who are *definitely* close to being able to re-establish their financial stability — provided they receive the proper guidance. Some of the issues Pa'amonim deals with are credit card debt, temporary or long-term job loss, unexpected illness and similar extraordinary circumstances. Pa'amonim could not do its work without knowing all the necessary details (including bank statements and similar documents) of the people with whom they are working. See **www.paamonim.com** for more details.

2. As their name indicates, Jewish free-loan societies offer interest-free loans. They also require certain knowledge about the borrower. (Free-loan societies are discussed at length in the chapter *Should I Accept Tzedakah Money If I Need It?*)

3. Millions of individuals and families have completely broken out of the cycle of poverty by receiving loans of as little as $50 or less. This kind of Tzedakah, known as "microloans", a concept invented by a single individual, Muhammad Yunus. The worldwide microloan movement is one of the great Tzedakah stories of the modern age, and billions of dollars have been successfully invested in people's lives with astonishing results. The incredibly wise *theory* of microloans coupled with the most remarkably well thought out *practical* process of distribution can leave you stunned, sometimes breathless, and occasionally saying to yourself, "Why didn't someone think of this hundreds of years ago?" Visit the following two websites to get the full story: **www.grameen-info.com** and **www.gfusa.org**. Obviously, the process of extending microloans to the appropriate recipients requires that anonymity be suspended.

To review: On Maimonides' scale of Tzedakah, it is the *second* level that requires anonymity. Both anonymous and non-anonymous Mitzvahs have their place. It all depends on the situation at hand, and in some of your Tzedakah work, you may want to do both kinds of Tikkun Olam.

On the Absolute Need to Talk About Your Tzedakah Work

There is an absolute need for you to talk about your Tzedakah work with others — family, friends, others exploring their own Tzedakah giving. Unfortunately, I believe that many people have taken Maimonides' 2nd level and extended it to mean that they should *never* tell anyone what they are doing with their Tzedakah money. Actually, there is an operative Jewish principle which supersedes the principle of secrecy — כדי לחנכו במצות-for the sake of Mitzvah education. This principle is mentioned in several different contexts in Talmudic literature and would most certainly apply to many areas of Tzedakah. In my opinion, there is a desperate need to share your Tzedakah knowledge and experience with others, so that they will not only be encouraged to do more of their own giving, but also so that they will have become more skilled at *how* they can give Tzedakah.

When you are telling about your own Tzedakah work, you should, of course, protect the anonymity of recipients. You will also need to decide whether or not to tell others *how much* you have given in each situation. But neither of these prevents you from telling others, "I have discovered these incredibly fine Mitzvah heroes (or Tzedakah organizations), have done all my due diligence and homework, checked them out 100%, and would like you to know more about them. And, as a result, I have given them some of my Tzedakah money to show that I believe in what they are doing." If you choose to do this, you will accomplish two things: (1) You may gain additional support for the people doing fine Tikkun Olam, and (2) you may prevent others from misdirecting funds to either inefficient or unworthy individuals or organizations.

However you do this — by personal conversation or by any other means at your disposal — you will be changing the direction of the trend that says, "What I do with my Tzedakah money is my own business."

When Secrecy and Anonymity Is a "Must'

You will encounter many situations where you want to *absolutely* keep your identity secret. A classic situation is when a relative, friend, or acquaintance is in need, and you want to offer financial support. Even beyond that circle of people, it could be anyone who might possibly know you and who would be embarrassed to find out that you had contributed. In that situation, your best option is a third party, such as a Tzedakah fund or Rabbi's discretionary fund, both of which can route the money to the recipient without any fear of your participation being discovered.

Briefly, the Thorny Question About Plaques

One extreme end of the scale is the joke about an institution's building that was made *entirely* out of donor's plaques. Not so far removed are places you have been where the walls are covered with names and categories of giving including "Angel", "President's Circle", "Builder", "Patron", and "Benefactor". Then there are institutions and organizations that restrict plaques to one small corner of the building. Finally, there are those that have no names whatsoever — not on the campus, the building, the program, not on a single plaque or certificate of recognition anywhere.

There is a similar scale of people's reactions to plaques and its related phenomenon, "naming opportunities" — from "none" to "as many as needed to bring in the money we need". You have your own view of what is in good taste and appropriate. More accurately, most likely you have a general opinion one way or another, but allow for specific exceptions. If you find this practice overdone, keep in mind that the plaque syndrome is not 100% about the ego-needs of the donor. Frequently donors will allow their names to be posted so that others who know them will be encouraged to join in the giving.

Whatever your personal opinion, it is important to mention that Jewish tradition *does* allow for public recognition of this kind. Ultimately, you yourself, will be the one to decide for if this is to be a part of your own way of giving — in the form of plaques, lists of donors in newsletters, websites, or similar forms of publicity, or some other non-anonymous venue.

How Does Jewish Tradition Define "Wealth"?

תנו רבנן: איזהו עשיר
כל שיש לו נחת רוח בעשרו דברי רבי מאיר
רבי טרפון אומר: כל שיש לו מאה כרמים ומאה שדות
ומאה עבדים שעובדין בהן
רבי עקיבא אומר: כל שיש לו אשה נאה במעשים
רבי יוסי אומר: כל שיש לו בית הכסא סמוך לשולחנו

Our Rabbis taught: Who is truly wealthy?
"Whoever gets satisfaction from his or her wealth, and feels at ease with
it," — the words of Rabbi Meir.
Rabbi Tarfon says, "Whoever has 100 vineyards and 100 fields and 100
workers working in them."
Rabbi Akiva says, "Whoever has a spouse whose deeds are pleasant and
pleasing."
Rabbi Yossi says, "Whoever has a bathroom near his or her dining room
table."

Shabbat 25b

All four answers have merit.

Rabbi Meir's answer is fairly self-explanatory. He is saying, "What good is having so much if it doesn't give you deep contentment?" The Hebrew term "נחת רוח-nachat ruach" actually means your "spirit is at rest, at peace with itself".

Rabbi Tarfon's answer seems too simplistic. In modern terms, the wealthy Rabbi Tarfon appears to answer, "Rich — someone with $4,000,000 in liquid assets, 20,000 shares of rock-solid stocks in your portfolio, a six-bedroom penthouse on the Upper East Side of New York, another in Palm Springs for the Winter, and a mansion on Dor Dor VeDorshav Street in Jerusalem." However, I am sure Rabbi Tarfon had more in mind when he gave his answer. I have studied this passage with many of my audiences, and they have offered several fine interpretations. The one I like the most is that Rabbi Tarfon feels rich because he can provide jobs for 100 people. Nevertheless, on its most straightforward level, his answer is the one you most expect to hear.

Rabbi Akiva's answer makes sense — to be blessed with an intimate partner whose salient characteristics are *Menschlichkeit* and involvement in Tikkun Olam.

My personal favorite, though, is Rabbi Yossi's. I think Rabbi Yossi is reacting to Rabbi Meir's and Rabbi Akiva's lofty responses. To Rabbi Yossi, you can have all the beauty and lyricism of what the other Rabbis taught, but for most people, taking care of the most fundamental matters of daily Life is what *really* makes you wealthy.

Should You Accept Tzedakah Money If You Need It?

Jewish tradition has a very clear position concerning making a living and the dignity of working to provide for one's own personal needs. To sustain oneself, a person should be willing to live sparingly if necessary, and should be prepared to do even menial work to be self-supporting. Three Talmudic texts teach:

ר' יהודה אמר: גדולה מלאכה שמכבדת את בעליה

Rabbi Yehuda said:
Work is noble — it gives dignity to the one who does it.   Nedarim 49b

רבי עקיבא היא דאמר: עשה שבתך חול ואל תצטרך לבריות

Rabbi Akiva said [referring to Shabbat meals]:
[If you have to], make your Shabbat [meal] like [those on] a week-day
rather than ask for assistance from others.   Shabbat 118a

כדאמר ליה רב לרב כהנא:
נטוש נבילתא בשוקא ושקול אגרא
ולא תימא גברא רבא אנא וזילא בי מילתא

Rav said to Rav Kahana:
[If you have to,] take a job flaying animal carcasses in the marketplace, take
your salary, but do not say, "I am a great man, and this is beneath my
dignity."   Bava Batra 110a

Indeed, many of the Talmudic Rabbis had humble occupations, including woodcutters and shepherds.

However, there are countless possible life situations when you might be unable to provide for yourself — either temporarily or permanently. What then? Based on Talmudic teachings, Maimonides unequivocally states Jewish tradition's position concerning taking Tzedakah when needed:

וכל מי שצריך ליטול ואינו יכול לחיות אלא אם כן נוטל
כגון זקן או חולה או בעל יסורין
ומגיס דעתו ואינו נוטל
הרי זה שופך דמים ומתחייב בנפשו
ואין לו בצערו אלא חטאות ואשמות

...and whoever needs to take Tzedakah, being unable to live without it —
such as an elderly person or one who is sick or is suffering greatly — and
who is too proud to take it — that person sheds blood and is to be held

accountable, and there is no benefit from the suffering...only sin and guilt.

Maimonides, Mishnah Torah,
Hilchot Matnot Ani'im, Laws of Gifts to Poor People, 10:19

This is in sharp contrast to the often-quoted, "I would rather die than take charity." Judaism opposes this for two reasons: (1) What comparative benefit would there be to have a dead human being as opposed to one who is alive and capable of doing good for others, and (2) "Charity" in this statement implies a "hand-out". "Tzedakah", as you know, means "doing the right thing", a much different concept. "Tzedakah" also means "entitlement"; the recipient is *entitled* to receive the Tzedakah money. "Tzedakah" carries no implication whatsoever of degrading the recipient. The recipient and giver are equals: two human beings, both entitled to a decent, dignified life. You are not "doing a favor" for the person in need. You are both mutually part of the system that makes for Tikkun Olam.

My friend, Brayton Campbell, stated it beautifully, "Asking for help is a compliment to the person you are asking; it is not a sign of weakness." If you are truly in need, you should not feel that, in some way, you are doing something wrong by accepting Tzedakah money or that this is *in any way* contrary to Jewish law. Quite the opposite: Accepting Tzedakah when you need it is *exactly* what Jewish law prescribes.

Jewish tradition provides a classic real-life example of being a recipient:

אבל אסור לאכול משלו בסעודה ראשונה

Mourners are not allowed to eat their own food at the first meal [after the funeral].

Shulchan Aruch, Yoreh De'ah 378:1

Several profound insights are contained in this brief statement. Among them are:

1. The mourner has returned home from a second traumatic loss — first the death of the loved one, and then the terribly stark scene of the burial itself. And more, he or she has to turn away from the grave, leave the loved one behind, and then return to familiar surroundings, now empty of the deceased's presence.

2. The mourner is emotionally weakened and lonely. Returning home, he or she finds that everything has been prepared — the low bench or stool to sit on, *and* the food. Everything has been made ready by friends and members of the mourner's community, using their own money to provide the meal.

3. This meal has a special name that, in itself, reveals the nature of the Mitzvah. It is called סעודת ההבראה-Se'udat HaHavra'ah, the Havra'ah meal. הבראה-Havra'ah, means "recovery, healing, restoration-to-health". True, the food is intended to provide physical nutrition. Of greater importance, though, is the fact that others are there for the mourner, to give the mourner strength by demonstrating that loneliness is *not* the human condition. People care, and they *insist* that the mourner know it, particularly at this most emotionally debilitating time in his or her personal life.

4. Perhaps most profound of all is Jewish tradition's assumption that the mourner is by nature a giving person. The lesson is: This is not the time to be a giver. The mourner *must* accept the community's acts of caring. Furthermore, knowing that the mourner is a giving person, tradition automatically frees him or her of the burden of having to ask others to help.

It just happens. No questions asked.

Two analogies will further explain Judaism's position about accepting Tzedakah. The first is obvious: An ambulance speeding through red lights and traveling well beyond the posted speed limit is not breaking the law. It is doing what the law says it has to do to save a life. The second relates to people who have to eat on Yom Kippur, which is what Jewish tradition demands. This is corroborated by a story I heard about the great Torah genius, Rabbi Chaim Soloveitchik of Brisk. He was once asked why he was so lenient about permitting sick people to eat on Yom Kippur. He replied, "I am not lenient. On the contrary, I am quite strict when it comes to the Mitzvah of saving lives." Rabbi Soloveitchik's teaching is clear: If you need to take, you *must* take…and it most certainly does not violate the norms of Judaism. To the contrary, *not* taking would be contrary to Jewish principles.

If you still have hesitations about accepting Tzedakah, you should be aware that there is an additional option — interest-free loans. Interest-free loans have existed in Jewish life since Biblical times (see Leviticus 25:35-38). Jewish free-loan societies are located in many communities around North America, some of them more than 100 years old. **www.freeloan.org** is the website of the IAHFL, The International Association of Hebrew Free Loans, and it can provide you with useful information if you want to explore this option. Each society has its own procedures for providing loans, but every aspect of the society's work relating to the person seeking the loan is done with absolute confidentiality. Depending on its resources, each one, also, offers a wider or narrower type of loan, such as for emergency needs, business loans, or support for education and job training.

If you *do* decide to explore this option, be aware of three important incontrovertible facts: (1) The individuals who operate free-loan societies are an amazing group of sensitive, caring people; (2) the statistics show that more than 95% (and often 99% or more) of the loans are paid back. This demonstrates that they are operating extremely effectively, and (3) some of the free loan societies are large operations, others very small — but no matter what size they are, they share a common operational rule: Everyone who comes to them is treated with the utmost dignity.

Can You *Really* Make Miracles Happen with *Your* Tzedakah Money?

Absolutely!

The story of Pharaoh's daughter and Moses and centuries of Jewish interpretation will serve as a classic example.

ותשלח את אמתה ותקחה

She [Pharaoh's daughter] sent her servant to take in the basket.

Exodus 2:5

The story:

1. Pharaoh decrees that all infant sons of the Israelite slaves are to be drowned in the Nile.

2. Moses' parents put the newborn in a basket and float it down the river.

3. Pharaoh's daughter goes down to bathe in the Nile, sees the basket with the infant inside, brings the child home, and raises him as a Prince of Egypt.

4. In the Divine Plan, he becomes God's emissary and leads the Children of Israel to freedom after centuries of slavery.

So reads the simple story in the Book of Exodus. The Torah wants us to understand that this chain of events was not mere chance, but rather *the hand of God* working miracles in history.

But later Jewish tradition teaches that there was another miracle involved. Rashi, based on a Talmudic Midrash (Sotah 12b), offers another interpretation. Since the Hebrew word "אמה-Ama" can also mean "arm", Exodus 2:5 *could* mean, "She [Pharaoh's daughter] *stretched out her arm* and took in the basket."

Menachem Mendel of Kotzk (1787-1859), one of the greatest Chassidic Rebbis, took this second meaning, and explained a most crucial element in the World of Mitzvahs. He said, "The boat was much farther from her than she could have ever possibly reached with her own arm. According to some Jewish interpretations, it was almost a hundred feet away when she saw it. But a miracle happened, and her arm became longer, long enough to reach the boat." The Kotzker continued, "But look — when she stretched out her arm, she had no idea that a miracle would happen. What could have possibly entered her mind to make her stretch out her arm to a place so far away that she couldn't [reasonably] reach it?" The Rebbi then taught that the real — the ultimate — human lesson is that "…this is the way of people who do good: Whether or not they can do it, they become so enthused about doing whatever good needs to be done, they don't sit around calculating whether or not they can actually succeed. The reward [for this kind of thinking-and-action] is that miracles *do* happen, and these people achieve even that which is commonly considered impossible."

If we wanted to give the Kotzker Rebbi's insightful teaching a name, we would call it "The Pharaoh's Daughter Principle". Simply put, if you think-and-act *for the sake of Mitzvahs*, if you stretch yourself *for the sake of Mitzvahs*, then miracles may very well happen. Were it not for Pharaoh's daughter, who extended herself to save the baby Moses, we would still be slaves in Egypt. One Mitzvah act changed the entire course of human history. This is most assuredly nothing less than a miracle.

There is a corollary to The Pharaoh's Daughter Principle: In relation to Tikkun Olam, logical thinking has its place, but it can take you only to a certain point. Besides the reasoned instructions from strategic planners and designers, you should be paying special attention to Mitzvah heroes, people who have learning disabilities, musicians and artists, teachers of small children, dreamers, day dreamers, visionaries, and anyone else who does not think the same way "normal" people do. From these teachers you may learn to be associative, dissociative, off-beat, out of the box, or wild in your thinking. It makes you free, just like the Children of Israel in ancient times. And as long as you thinking is *thinking-for-the-sake-of-doing-Mitzvahs*, nothing but Good will come of it, sometimes far more good than you ever anticipated.

And there is a second corollary, taught to me by my friend, student, and teacher, Miriam Heller. I quote from her note to me: "Following your sentences about thinking 'normally', again, my mind ran off in a different direction. The slaves who left Egypt did not survive the 40-year journey through the desert. Only the next generation could enter the Promised Land, a generation who knew not of the slave mentality, who could think and act like free people. In this age, we also need to raise a new generation — one that will feel free to think differently than the generation that preceded it — out of the box, non-linearly. A generation that will be idealistic, that won't be jaded by bureaucracy, that won't take no for an answer."

Miriam has made a most significant point, but I would not want anyone to think that the "new generation" refers only to young people. *Anyone* is capable of being untainted by the thinking of "It can't be done" and "That's just the way the world is". All it takes is to remember Pharaoh's daughter, and to find the right teachers to teach you elementary and advanced Mitzvah thinking.

Is It Possible to Do a "Pure" Act of Tzedakah With Your Money?

Yes.

Absolutely.

Having said that, the essential Tzedakah question is, "How do you determine if what you did with your Tzedakah money was a pure act of Tzedakah?"

I believe there are two criteria for determining the purity of the act: *motive* and *expectation of return.* Your possible *motive* for doing Tzedakah — because it is a Mitzvah, because you feel good, because it helps others, out of guilt or pity, etc. — is discussed in other parts of this guide. As for *expectation of return*, the Jewish answer is relatively simple: You should expect no thank-you from the recipient(s) and no public recognition for what you have done.

One Jewish text relates a curious and somewhat extreme tale of Tzedakah. (Jerusalem Talmud, Pe'ah, Chapter 8, end of Halachah 7) To paraphrase the story: One day, Rabbi Elazar came home and asked the members of his family what kind of Tzedakah they had done while he was gone. They answered that a group of hungry people had come by, and they had fed them. In gratitude, the wayfarers had prayed for Rabbi Elazar's continued wellbeing. The Rabbi was not at all pleased and told the family members that there was no good reward for their act. Another time he came home and asked the same question. They gave the same answer, but this time the guests had *cursed* the Rabbi. The Rabbi told the members of his family that *that* kind of response indicated that their Mitzvah-act had been pure.

Again, this is certainly an extreme example. Nevertheless, in the same section of the Talmud, the following is told:

ר"ע בעין ממניתיה פרנס
א"ל נמלך גו ביתא
הלכון בתריה שמעון קליה דימור
על מנת מקל על מנת מבזייא

Members of his community wanted to appoint Rabbi Akiva manager of the community's Tzedakah fund.
He said to them, "I want to go home and consult with the members of my family."
They followed him [to his home] and overheard,
"[Know that you] will be humiliated and maligned."

The language of the ancient text is problematical. "פרנס-Parnass" can mean either "community leader" or "manager of the community's Tzedakah funds." It is also possible that the closing line means that Rabbi Akiva said to his family, "I am accepting this position fully aware that I may be humiliated and maligned", and thereby telling them not to be concerned about the criticisms that will possibly come with the position.

Still, it would seem natural that the recipient ought to show *some* appreciation for what you have done. You should keep in mind, though, that there are several legitimate reasons why some kind of "thank-you" might not be forthcoming. While your initial reaction may be that the recipient is ungrateful, that is certainly not always true. Some of the following circumstances may explain the reason for the silence:

1. The recipients may be too embarrassed to respond. This is a common and very real aspect of the relationship of recipients to donors. *It happens all the time.*

2. To preserve their own dignity, the recipients just cannot communicate with the giver in any way.

3. By their very nature, the recipients may just be inarticulate people or, unable to express themselves.

4. The recipients, even though generally articulate, may be experiencing "first-time recipient syndrome". They have never had to take from others before, and, in addition, they may have never had to *ask* for anything from others before.

5. There may have been some glitch in communication. You know this from everyday life — for whatever reason, a letter just never got to you, or an e-mail got lost in cyberspace or disappeared when your computer crashed. It is possible that some Mitzvah-intermediary — perhaps the person who delivered the furniture you anonymously bought for a family in need — forgot to tell you that the single mother expressed appreciation what you had done for her family.

6. Furthermore, the recipients may have profound psychological scars which you could not possibly comprehend, even if you were the most skilled therapist. (In this situation you most certainly can understand why the recipients do *not* express their gratitude.)

All of these are valid possibilities, but whatever the reason or reasons, "thank you" is not *your* issue. It is enough for you to know that you recognized another person's need, responded to it, and did the right thing by using your money for an act of Tzedakah.

Postscript: A New Term

In the realm of Gemillut Chassadim, i.e., using your non-monetary effort, time, or talents for others, there is a particularly rich Jewish term, חסד של אמת-Chessed shel Emet, a true act of caring lovingkindness. The Talmud explains that burying someone is a Chessed shel Emet because there is absolutely no possibility of a return, reward, or thank-you from that person. What is described above about Tzedakah money would then be צדקה של אמת-Tzedakah shel Emet, true, pure Tzedakah.

Will Your Tzedakah Money Have a Greater Impact If You Give Larger Amounts to a Single Tikkun Olam Program Rather Than Smaller Amounts to Many?

Sometimes yes and sometimes no.

For Small Sums — Part I – the "No":

Your pattern of giving may include giving at least some small amount of Tzedakah every time you are asked. This may include personal solicitations, phone calls, e-mails, or snail-mail requests. The importance of doing research about these solicitations is covered in other chapters in this book. Those selections will cover how to prevent an unreasonably large percentage of your Tzedakah dollar from being wasted. This chapter is concerned with donating small sums to Mitzvah heroes and organizations you have already researched.

For Small Sums — Part II — the "Yes":

When you have discovered Mitzvah heroes and programs that change the lives of others for the better with $5.00, $2.00, $1.00, even 50¢ — then making many small donations is entirely appropriate. And more — not only is it entirely appropriate, it should become a regular facet of your personal Tzedakah program.

The next chapter — *What Possible Difference Could $38.00, $22.00, $18.00 — Even $2.66 — Make in Someone's Life?* — discusses in detail how small sums of Tzedakah money *can* and *do* make miracles happen. Keep in mind that becoming accustomed to this aspect of Tzedakah also serves as a constant reminder of the awesome power of Mitzvah money to do incredible quantities of good.

For Large Sums:

Suppose you want to buy school supplies or provide hot lunches for a group of students whose families do not have enough money. And, let us say you have done your research and are satisfied that the organization is doing the program economically and efficiently. If the group says that the program will not happen at all unless X dollars are collected, then it makes sense to contribute all, or a large percentage of, your Tzedakah budget to this one worthy program. If, however, you have done your research and "something doesn't feel right" about what you have discovered, even if you have enormous sums to give away, then, even though the absolute value of your Tzedakah money may be very high —

$25,000, $100,000, $1,000,000 — the true Tikkun Olam value may fall to near-zero or absolute nil.

To give an extreme example: According to Beth Healy's article in *The Boston Globe* (1/27/04) entitled, "6 Harvard endowment managers earn combined total of $107.5m", the fund was worth $19,300,000,000 at that time, a gain of more than $700,000,000 over the previous year. One bond manager was paid $35,100,000, up from $15,900,000 the previous year, and another received $34,100,000, almost double the previous year's salary. The president of the investment group stated that the managers deserved "every penny" of what they were paid. It is your personal choice, of course, to decide whether or not this is a fiscally responsible use of a university's endowment money. If you consider it inappropriate, then your large donation would be better used elsewhere, as for example…

You could allow Libby Reichman's Big Brothers Big Sisters of Jerusalem to triple the number of at-risk children it reaches. For decades into the future, many lives could be changed. "Many lives" means not only the lives of the "Little Brothers" and "Little Sisters", but also the lives of thousands of others they will encounter over those future years of living a better life. *Their* lives, too, will be better because of your well-timed and well-placed Tzedakah. (**www.bigbrothers.org.il/EngVersion**)

And, as for example: You could make the dreams come true for hundreds or thousands of Elders in closed-care institutions by donating and working with PK Beville and Second Wind Dreams. (**www.secondwind.org**)

And, as for example: If you (1) are very thorough in your research, (2) find a Mitzvah hero whose Tikkun Olam work appeals to you spiritually, existentially, and intellectually, and (3) you don't necessarily need to worry about tax deductions, then you can call that Mitzvah hero and say, "What can $50,000 do for you?" Give and take and refine the match of needs to funds, then just do it.

And, as for example…

And, as for example…

By then, you will be "on a roll" and one glorious Mitzvah will lead to another and to another and to yet another.

In Sum: How Much Is a "Large Sum"? a "Small Sum"? and What About "Medium Sums?"

Your personal understanding of "small sums" and "large sums" will depend on your own Tzedakah budget. (And depending on that absolute figure, you will also be able to determine how much is available in the category of "medium sums".)

Most likely, you will want to do all kinds of Tzedakah — small and medium, and large, if "large" is within your range. All amounts of Tzedakah money *will* and *do* change lives, and all — when done right — are equally valid. *Every* Tzedakah dollar has the power to change lives for the better, and, indeed, to make miracles happen.

What Possible Difference Could
$38.00, $22.00, $18.00 — Even $2.66 —
Make in Someone Else's Life?

וצדקה תציל ממות

Tzedakah saves from death.

Proverbs 10:2

If You Have Already Read the Chapter about People Who Have More Money Than God

— Then

You may be feeling frustrated or inadequate. You may be thinking that the only way to change the world is with millions, billions, or gazillions of dollars. Don't despair and don't even think twice about it. There are not only as many ways to do Tikkun Olam with small sums of money as there are by huge sums, in reality, there are *many* more of them. I dropped out of college math after two semesters of calculus, so I am not certain if there are *infinitely* more. But there are many, many, *many* more.

Report from Arnie Draiman

Arnie Draiman is Ziv Tzedakah Fund's representative in Israel. We exchange e-mails many times a day, with phone calls scattered over time depending on the need. Among other things, he loves to play a role in small-money high-impact Mitzvahs. When I told him I was considering doing a short piece about $5.00, $10.00, $25.00 Mitzvahs, he sent me the following report. It is unedited, except for certain details that he and I changed to preserve the confidentiality and anonymity of the recipients:

Real live ones in the last several months:

under $100 —
$72 - winter electric bill for elderly person ([we do] many elec bills for many people)
$61 - phone bill for survivor of terror ([we do] many phone bills)
$96 - pair of comfortable sneakers for survivor of terror (with foot pain)
$85 -taking a small family of a survivor out to dinner - woman so enthralled by actually going out again she stayed up the night before sewing/making a new dress for the "occasion"
$78 - good chair for a desk for a college student survivor of terror
$55 - school uniforms for kids from survivor of terror family
$85 - for new holiday clothes

$80 - grocery scrip (can come in any amount)

under $50 —
$43 - shoes for a kid at Bet Hayeled (*www.geocities.com/bhayeled/*)
$40 - toys for kid survivors of terror for Chanukah
$38 - gas heating bill for survivor of terror
$50 - for balloons and chocolate to kid after operation

under $25 —
$18 for balloons for another kid after operation
$4 -dreidls and chocolate for kid for Chanukah at a shelter for victims of domestic
   violence (x 30 for a group, but that was the per price)

A Very Special $22.00 Mitzvah

This is an e-mail we received from one of our other "inside contacts" in Israel. Again, details have been changed to safeguard the identity and dignity of the recipients:

H called me to ask if I had anything to do with the flowers they received. She was so thrilled and said that she couldn't figure out who would have known about them other than me. She said they were beautiful and made them feel good. Their father was killed in a פיגוע-pigua [terrorist attack] and their mother died of one of those terrible diseases and the daughters are all in their late teens and early 20s totally on their own.

Infant Thermometers

One of Ziv Tzedakah Fund's Mitzvah heroes, Jeannie Jaybush, is working with so many poor people in Seattle it is hard to keep track of everything she does. Often, when confronted with an endless stream of possibilities and only a finite amount of Tzedakah money to give, we review her wish list with her, and we pick one or two items we can afford to purchase for her.

In the recent past she told us about the need for infant thermometers for families to have on hand at home. And then she told us a very sad story. A newborn child had been running a fever, but because the parents were illegal immigrants, they were afraid to take the infant to the emergency room. As time went on, it was clear that the child was suffering. When the visiting nurse arrived and examined the infant, the parents knew they that had to take the risk. By the time the emergency room people could take care of the child, it became clear that the child had meningitis and because of the long delay had suffered permanent damage.

This didn't have to happen. Now, our search was on for getting good prices for bulk orders of thermometers…and people to donate the money to pay for them. Ziv found contributors to cover most of the cost, then paid for the rest. Naomi Eisenberger, Ziv's Managing Director, searched for a good price and discovered that we could buy dozens at approximately $3.50 apiece. Ziv bought substantial quantities at that price. Particularly moving was the fact that the students of the early childhood department of a synagogue school donated a significant portion of the money to pay for many of the thermometers.

That was months ago.

More recently, someone remembered Jeannie's need and Naomi's quest for a good price, and the son of a good friend came through with an even better price. For $2,000, Ziv could buy approximately 780 thermometers. Adding $75.00 for shipping, that unit price came to about $2.66 apiece.

For $2.66, maybe years of suffering have been avoided for hundreds of children.

For $2.66.

Infinitely More

Perhaps what I wrote in the opening paragraph is wrong. Maybe there really are *infinitely* more $38.00, $25.00, $10.00, and $2.66 Mitzvahs waiting to happen Out There if you seek them out. It would be nice to have more, as much, or almost as much money as God, but even if you don't, there is just *so* much you can do.

Just imagine — $2.66 can save a life!

How Should You Do Tzedakah
If You Happen to Have More Money Than God,
or As Much, or Almost As Much Money As God?
You Could...

You could wipe out a disease that ravages millions of people's lives. Bill and Melinda Gates and Bono have taken the initiative in this vast area of Tikkun Olam.

You could join them in this effort.

You can make sure that every kid in your community gets a free Jewish day school education.

You can.

You might fund 50,000 people to be tested as potential bone marrow donors. Each one just might save a life.

You could establish institutes in Israel and North America to train people in doing Earthshaking Tzedakah. The program would focus on students meeting Mitzvah heroes, learning from these Distinguished Teachers of Tikkun Olam, and then joining them in their work. Your budget could cover not only constructing and maintaining the buildings, but also setting up an endowment. The staff could then do its holy work without ever needing to worry about raising funds for operations. The total package probably wouldn't take more than $5,000,000 or $10,000,000.

You could do it.

You could do it if that's what appeals to you.

It might even be "a piece of cake" for you.

You could travel to Israel and ask every one of the Mitzvah heroes what they need to make *every one* of their dreams come true. And not just their temporary or mid-range measures to gain stability just for now. For the ones who are inspired and inspiring but can't seem to do anything administrative, you can buy them assistants and infrastructure so that they can be *totally* left to do what they do best, namely, change lives according to their vision and talents. For example, you could build a facility for Anita Shkedi and her Israel National Therapeutic Riding Association (INTRA), and provide for *all* her other needs: additional staff to manage the operation, *and* provide enough money where she could advertise, "Let all those in need of body-and-soul repair come to us." (**www.intra.org.il**)

You could, if that appeals to you. It certainly is a critical need.

And you could do it without any desire to exert personal control, because you know the Mitzvah heroes will make wise use of your money.

You could just walk into the home of a Mitzvah hero whose Tikkun Olam work you have researched carefully, hand over a check for $1,000,000 — no questions asked — then ride off into the sunset on your white horse with a mighty "Hi ho, Silver, away!"

You could establish a new Mitzvah program to replace one that is too inefficient or wasteful.

You could, and you would feel very good about it, because you were making it happen more efficiently, more economically, and more people would have better lives because of it.

You could pick up the phone and call a friend who also has more than, as much as, or nearly as much money as God and say, "Sophie, please sit down with Miriam and tell her that I am putting in $4,000,000 for Jewish Elders in the Former Soviet Union. Massive numbers of them are living on $30- and $40-a-month pensions. I want to give them the kind of money that will let them get their medicines, better food, a chance to go outside for a stroll in the Springtime…and a chance to be happy. Discuss it, but don't discuss it to death. I already have the perfect Mitzvah hero who can reach hundreds of people, so there won't be any worry about anything going to waste. See if she likes the idea and if the two of you would like to match my $4,000,000." (Visit www.amechad.org and learn of Igor Feldblyum's fine work in this area of Tikkun Olam.)

You could do it. Millionaires and billionaires do it all the time, and you could feel "double extra" good because you have doubled your Mitzvah money by making just one phone call.

Whatever it is, do it because (1) it is something that you *personally* like, (2) it is desperately needed, or, best of all, (3) you have reached a point in your Tzedakah giving to realize it has to be some combination of (1) and (2). With that much money you have already come to realize that it isn't enough just to base your miracle-work on personal preference. There has to be something more.

You Could Do it <u>With</u> the Help of

People who "get it", i.e.:.,

…people who know how Tzedakah money works miracles and changes the lives of people in need

…people who have the human touch

…people who are constantly aware that, while your endeavors are potentially dripping with all the pitfalls of a "power trip", they have a firm grip on the truth: Tikkun Olam is humbling and, Fixing the World is all about humility

…people who "get" who *you* are, always respect your own Self, and never overstep their bounds when helping you to put your Tzedakah money to work best.

You certainly could do Tzedakah better with these fine people at your side.

You Could Do It _Without_ the Help of

...some social investment entrepreneurs who have brought the good message of sound business management to Mitzvah work, _but_ who may have gone too far in their theoretical transfer of principles. They may have forgotten that Mitzvah work and business principles don't _always_ overlap. They may not be focusing enough on _human_ needs. There may be occasions when "risk" means something different. They may not have had enough experience in Tikkun Olam to understand that "cost effectiveness" is often, _but not always_, a primary consideration. It is possible that, when it comes to Mitzvahs, they haven't yet grasped the proper balance between rational long-term planning and "gut feeling". Many times they do it out of innocence, but, whatever the reason, you will probably do better without their help if they seem too absolutist about their theories.

...a few — probably more than a few — people who make their living by slick presentations to people just like yourselves. They are the ones you read about who scan the newspapers for lottery winners. Some are expert hucksters, and others are classic shysters and frauds. No doubt you can do a lot better without them if they suddenly appear at your door.

No doubt, you have already given away serious money to Tzedakah. Along the way you may have been burned once or twice. Be aware that there _are_ many people who can work with you that do not fall into any of the previous categories.

A Story: Paul Newman

Think about Paul Newman, actor, director, race car driver...and Big Time Tzedakah Man. By 2006, he had given away more than $200,000,000. Everyone knows the story:

"Gee, Paul, you ought to sell this yummy salad dressing of yours."

"I'll do it, but let's take all of the money I make and give it away to Tzedakah."

Read the labels on his products. There's a nice touch of humor to each one. You see it at **www.newmansown.com** and other resources. "Paul Newman, as sole owner of Newman's Own™, donates all his after-tax profits to educational and charitable purposes." Nice, but even nicer is the line, "Newman's Own: Shameless Exploitation In Pursuit of The Common Good." It's the same style of humor that we remember from _Butch Cassidy and The Sundance Kid_. Paul contributes to hundreds of Tzedakah projects. I haven't checked lately, but, a few years ago, I read an article that reported he is _directly_ involved in the giving, and that the Newman's Own Tzedakah staff has a good sense of how to do it. But even allowing for a 2% or 3% "unwise staff hiring" record, he has done much better than others who don't have quite as much money as God, but still enough to do a multitude of divine Mitzvahs.

A Second Story: Eugene Lang

More than 20 years ago, Eugene Lang was asked to give a speech to a 6th grade graduating class. The school was in East Harlem where he, himself, had been a student years before. In the interim, the neighborhood had changed and the student population was composed mostly of disadvantaged and at-risk kids. Shortly before Mr. Lang delivered his talk, he had a revelation. He set aside his prepared speech, and, instead, spoke from the heart. He promised that he would send any students to college who would graduate from high school.

The "I Have a Dream Foundation" was born, and its website, which reviewed the background for the 1995 Presidential Medal of Freedom that he received states, "IHAD currently supports 150 projects in 57 cities nationwide. More than 200 sponsors have helped more than 12,000 disadvantaged students with academic support and guidance from elementary school through their high school years."

I still haven't met Mr. Lang. Nor have I met Paul Newman (though I drove by his house once). They're both on my "Some Day" calendar. Soon, I hope.

Extreme Wealth

You know the stories about various idiosyncrasies and often severely-misplaced values of some super-wealthy people. Recently, I heard one from a friend. He told me about a woman who had millions in the bank, and a money market fund with more than $500,000. She used this account for writing personal checks. My friend told me that this woman would fly into an absolute panic when the account dipped below $500,000. She was terrified that she was running out of ready cash.

There are tales in every body of literature about rich people who are very stingy when it comes to Tzedakah. One of my favorite Chassidic stories is about a Rebbi who summons a rich man to his house to teach a lesson about giving. First he takes him to a window and asks, "What do you see?"

The rich man replies, "I see some people taking a leisurely stroll. Others are going into shops and buying things. To the right are some kids playing in the square."

The Rebbi then takes him to a mirror and asks, "What do you see?"

The rich man answers, "I see myself."

The Rebbi then says, "See — the window is made of glass, but add a little silver to it, and you stop seeing other people. You see only yourself."

As I said, when I was writing this chapter, I wasn't even thinking of the classic "stingy rich person" theme. There are just too many people out there with oodles, tons, and semi-truckloads of money who are making Mitzvahs happen Big Time.

One Final Thought

You may be one of the few who has millions, tens of millions, hundreds of millions, or a billion or two at your disposal. I have had some contact with individuals such as yourselves, and I would only add this: While you are thinking about and doing Very Big Mitzvahs, keep in mind that you can also make some "small" or medium-size Tikkun Olam happen. There is a certain fascination about giving away a million here and a million there, but also remember to be on the look-out for opportunities where $10,000, $25,000 or $50,000 will make *the* difference. For you, it may be no more difficult than just writing a check. But for the Mitzvah hero and his or her work, for other Tikkun Olam programs, or for other recipients, it will save hours, weeks, perhaps months of work, anguish, and unnecessary suffering. This is just one more aspect of your Mitzvah work that can give you a unique sense of satisfaction.

There are, of course, in addition a hefty number of situations where $100, $180, $250, or $500 could change someone's life completely.

Indeed, your Tzedakah work could be very rich, combining Colossal-Sized Tzedakah, Medium-Range Tzedakah, and Small Tzedakah (which never is "small". Never.)

You could do it. No doubt about it.

The only thing left to do is to do it.

One More Final Thought

eMarketer is a website devoted to "daily coverage of the latest e-business data and eMarketer analysis." A May 19, 2005, report stated that Baby Boomers have $1,000,000,000,000 (that's $1 trillion) in buying power. Other sources estimate an even more staggering figure. As best as I can tell, whatever the precise number might be, it sounds like "almost as much money as God has" in the celestial bank at any one time. The writer is, of course, referring to the classical definition of "Baby Boomer", i.e., Americans born between 1946 and 1964. He doesn't break it down by age sub-groups, but I would suspect that even a small percentage of $1 trillion held by the older Boomers can do an incredible amount of Tikkun Olam.

Why Is There No Blessing (ברכה-Bracha) Recited Before Doing an Act of Tzedakah?

Sometimes it seems that there is a special blessing for everything in Judaism: before eating a sandwich, when celebrating a momentous event in Life, on week-days, Shabbat, and holidays, seeing a rainbow, landing in Israel…The list goes on and on. It is true that there are several Mitzvah acts and occasions for which there is no prescribed blessing. Nevertheless, many people I talk to find it particularly curious why there is no Bracha before doing an act of Tzedakah. You would think that, for such an important Jewish and human action, it should be honored or sanctified by a blessing of praise or thanks. Over the past several years, I have asked dozens of people why they think this is so. Usually, I get the best answers when I ask the question "out of the blue". This allows them to give their first spontaneous answer.

In no particular order, some of the answers I have received include:

1. If you are concentrating on making the blessing, you may be interfering with giving your Tzedakah properly and efficiently. Or you may be so focused on doing the act of Tzedakah just right, you may make a mistake when you recite the blessing. Both of these are particularly true for people who often have to grope and fumble to remember the right words or who are not skilled "multi-taskers".

2. Probably the most powerful one I have heard: There are times when there is not a second to lose. Many Tzedakah situations require an immediate response. Delay of any kind may have serious consequences, including embarrassment to the person in need or even loss of life because of that split-second delay. The need to be prepared at all times is illustrated by a Talmudic story about the sage Rabbi Chana bar Chanila'i

ולא שקל ידא מן כיסא דסבר דילמא אתי עני בר טובים
ואדמטו לי לכיסא קא מכסיף

who always kept a hand in his pocket, thinking, "A poor person who was once financially stable may come along, and by the time I reach into my pocket to give, the person may feel humiliated." Berachot 58b

3. A psychological approach: Since it often seems that giving money away goes against the grain of human nature, there is no need to recite a blessing. You are taking this most common and frequently-misused thing — money — and using it for a holy purpose. How could you *not* know that this act is something special? Therefore, my interpreter-friend explained, there is no need for a Bracha to remind you that you are engaged in something sacred.

4. There is the slightest chance that personal pride *may* intrude when you are engaged in an act of Tzedakah. You *might* think, "I [i.e., Big Me, Look at me!]

am going to do something so important that there is even a Bracha assigned to it". That would shift the focus too much to the donor, rather than to the recipient.

5. My friend and teacher, Rabbi Neal Gold, made reference to a Torah-insight by the Chassidic Rebbi Simcha Bunem. The Rebbi taught that one who needs to make a Bracha may not consider himself or herself "clean" enough to pronounce such holy words. Therefore, there is no Bracha, and the person should respond immediately to the need. Rabbi Gold offers three contemporary interpretations of "not 'clean' enough": 1) lacking the self-confidence to make a difference, (2) lacking the perspective that one *is* capable of making a difference, and (3) thinking to one's self, "There are others who do this so much better than I do." Therefore, Rabbi Bunem is saying, "Remove all hesitation, doubt, and comparisons, and *do* something."

6. My friend and teacher, Louise Cohen, sent me a particularly eloquent and profound possible answer:

> In general, Brachas make us more conscious of God's gifts to us, so we pause to sanctify moments in time, food, etc. But maybe it's better not to be so "conscious" of the fact that we are giving Tzedakah. Champion figure skaters and other athletes talk about "skating dumb" and "muscle memory". By the time they are in competition, they stop "thinking", intellectualizing, and analyzing what they need to do to perform their amazing leaps and spins. It becomes not just <u>what they do</u> but also <u>who they are</u>. Similarly, giving Tzedakah should become part of what we do and who we are. Instead of wasting time verbalizing the holiness of the act, we should just do it. We say blessings at the beginning of each day, thanking G-d for making us who we are, then we go about our day. Ideally, we could say a blessing before the gift of each brand new breath we inhale and exhale, but that wouldn't be a sane way to live. Just as we are creatures that live by breathing in and out — and our other blessings acknowledge that we don't take this for granted — we should also be creatures for whom giving Tzedakah is an organic, almost biological component of who we are, and it is covered under our general daily blessings.

These six interpretations barely scratch the surface. Perhaps it would be beneficial now and again to ask ourselves the same question, "Why is there no blessing before doing an act of Tzedakah?" Each new answer yields new meanings, and each one enriches the experience and adds to the power of the act itself.

Exactly
How Do You Decide
Where to Donate
Your Tzedakah Money?

Is It Enough That "They" Are Doing Good Things – Why Should Trustworthiness Be Your Ultimate Concern When You Donate Your Money to Tzedakah?

The short answer is, "No."

When I review the many letters and e-mails I get from rabbis, educators, and friends that report where they have sent their Tzedakah money, two questions come to my mind:

1. Is it enough that the organizations that receive their Tzedakah money are doing good things, or is there something more that we should expect from them?

2. Have the rabbis, educators, and friends done their homework? By this I mean — did they check the organizations out sufficiently, i.e., do they *really* know *exactly* what these recipient-groups will be doing with the Tzedakah money they are soliciting? The short answer to this one is "often they do not."

Both of these are crucial issues, and will be discussed in subsequent chapters.

What Is the Fundamental Jewish Text About Trust?

Common sense should tell you that you would want and need to know how your money is being used. This is true in both areas where money makes a difference, i.e., money for your own personal needs, and, no less, for Tzedakah.

Let us say some of the lights begin to flicker in your house. You call the electrician, settle on the cost, and this expert examines and repairs what needs to be fixed. When the process is over, you will want to know not only that everything works properly, but also that the house is safe from an electrical fire. That is what you paid for. Consequently, you can go to the beach or visit your favorite Uncle Sholom Dov for a week without fear that the house will be destroyed because of some mishap in your home's wiring system. That is what you paid for.

It makes sense.

Tzedakah works the same way. You want to change the world by making someone else's life, in some way, better than it is. You will then begin to search for a Mitzvah hero, an organization, or a cause that does just that — makes lives better. Because so much is at stake, you will most definitely want to make certain that the people you are dealing with are absolutely reliable.

It makes sense.

It is simple logic, *common* sense.

My friend, Sharon Halper, gave this procedure a name — The Rule of the Three E's: Is any recipient of your Tzedakah going to use the money *efficiently* and *effectively*, and will they use it *exactly* as they said they would.

Jewish tradition has considerable literature concerning the responsibility of the donor and the recipient. Maimonides' summarizes it in his Mishnah Torah Law Code (Laws of Gifts to Poor People, Chapter 10):

ולא יתן אדם לתוך קופה של צדקה
אלא אם כן יודע שהממונה נאמן וחכם ויודע להנהיג כשורה...

...one should not give to a Tzedakah fund unless the donor knows that the person responsible is נאמן-trustworthy, wise [in managing and distributing the funds], and acts with the absolute integrity...

To understand the full implications of this text, it is best to break it down into two areas: (1) the managers, board of directors, and any others involved in collecting and distributing the funds and directing the program activities, and (2) the organization's overall finances. This is discussed in detail in the chapter *How Do You Evaluate Financial Information from a Tzedakah Program So That You Can Decide to Whom to Give or Not to Give?*

Why Is the Hebrew Root "אמן-Amen" the Same As for "נאמן-Ne'eman", "Trustworthy"

The Same?

אמן-Amen.

You have heard the word since you were a child. And you hear it everywhere. You hear it in synagogue (where you would expect to hear it) and you hear it outside of the sanctuary walls. You are not surprised to hear a talk show host respond to a caller by saying, "Ay-men to that, buddy."

Being a student of words, I began to look into the meaning of this very short, very powerful word. It didn't take long before I discovered that its essential meaning is "firm, strong", and saying "Amen" meant that we confirm or affirm what someone else had just said, proclaimed, or offered in prayer. Digging a little deeper, I learned that אמן-Amen is related to ימן – the root of the word "ימין-right hand". Throughout the millennia-long history of the Hebrew language, this word became a synonym for "strength, power". Other languages also favored the right hand. In Latin, "dexter" eventually became "dextrous" in English. The French, "droite" became our "adroit", skillful. The opposite — "left" — developed negative connotations. In Latin it is "sinister", in French, "gauche". You need only ask Elders if any of them who were born left-handed were forced by their parents to write with their right hand.

"Right" is good; "left" is to be avoided at all costs.

This is exactly why "אמן" and its cousin "ימן" are so important in the world of Tzedakah. Maimonides' text quoted in a previous chapter gives three crucial criteria for those in charge of any Tzedakah program: They must be נאמנים-trustworthy, wise [in managing and distributing the funds], and must act with absolute integrity. You would want to add, also, that the supervisors are Menschen and treat the recipients *and their employees* decently and fairly.

Even without any reference to Jewish texts, it should be obvious why you would want to know about the character of the directors and the staff members who manage Tzedakah money. You have to *trust* them. This Mitzvah money is meant to better the lives of others. More than your plumber or car mechanic, they *have* to know what they are doing because the stakes are so high. They have the power of life and death no less than the heart surgeon who replaces a damaged valve. And, not least of all, they ought to be the kind of person you like and respect as a human being.

How Do You Evaluate Financial Information from a Tzedakah Program So That You Can Decide to Whom to Give or Not to Give?

If you are giving to an organization, you are entitled to see a copy of its financial report. The Jewish reasoning is relatively simple. As explained in other chapters of this book, Tzedakah money is never "owned" by the donor. Rather, that portion of our income that is intended for Tzedakah is entrusted to us by God to reach appropriate recipients. If we are trustees, Jewish tradition teaches we should certainly be *responsible* trustees.

In a situation where you know the organization 100% top-to-bottom and backwards-and-forwards, then you may want to get a copy of the budget as a simple formality and point of reference. This is one of the wonderful advantages I have enjoyed over 30 years working with Mitzvah heroes. Since the Mitzvah heroes are absolutely trustworthy, examining the finances is relatively easy. If, however, you do not know the organization, or know them for their work but do not know their finances, ask for the "numbers". Of course, if they balk and do not want to send you any documentation, Judaism frees you from any obligation to give to them.

When you *do* get a copy of its finances, ask yourself, how do the figures of the non-profit generally look to you?

1. How much is the **overhead**? This is the essential word — *overhead*, costs of running the operation, salaries, fundraising expenses, publicity, office expenses, and the like.

2. How much is spent on fundraising, publicity, and similar items in relation to how much actually goes to the stated programs of the Tzedakah fund?

3. Is the financial sheet easily understandable?

4. If individuals receive salaries, do they seem reasonable to you?

5. After you have read and reviewed the financial statements, if you still have any questions, contact the organization directly. Ask yourself, were you satisfied that you received timely, straightforward, and complete answers?

Without any of the above information, you should not be giving to that fund. Today, the word "transparency" is used when referring to a non-profit's financial statements. Is it all clear, easily accessible, and without detours or obfuscating terminology and explanations? As always, if there are any doubts, you should be checking with the people behind the financial reports directly for clarification.

There is one other step you should take: Surf the internet to check if there have been any articles — positive or negative — about your potential recipients. There may be something "out there" which you need to know before you contribute.

For your reference, the first mention of financial accountability is in the Bible. Concerning repairs and maintenance of the Temple in King Josiah's time, II Kings 22:7 states:

אך לא=יחשב אתם הכסף הנתן על ידם כי באמונה הם עשים

> *...but no accounting was done concerning the donations given, because they did their work in a trustworthy manner.*

Over the course of time, Jewish tradition changed its approach. Rabbi Moshe Isserles, basing his decision on an earlier ruling, adds the following comment to a law in the 16th century Shulchan Aruch code:

הגה ומ"מ כדי שיהיו נקיים
הגה מה' ומישראל טוב להם ליתן חשבון

> *In any event, it is best for them [the managers of the Tzedakah fund] to give an accounting so that they stay "clean" — [as the verse states in Numbers 32:22], "...you shall be untainted both as far as God and Israel are concerned".*

The following chapters will provide additional details that will help you determine how to read and understand the finances, efficiency, and accountability of organizations that you might consider supporting.

What Is "Easy" Money?

As described in other chapters, when you are deciding who are appropriate recipients for your Tzedakah money, you need to examine "the numbers". You will be looking into both overhead percentages, and also *absolute* numbers. "Absolute numbers" simply means how much money the group, organization, or cause has raised and how much has been distributed. While both of these are crucial facts to keep in mind, there is an additional element to remember: "easy" money. Two examples will clarify:

1. Word has gotten out by various means that a child needs a heart transplant. The cost is $500,000, even with doctors donating their services. In general, this is "easy" money, as people will readily respond to the call to save a child's life, and money may very well come pouring in. Occasionally it is "easier" money because the appeal is being publicized through a well-connected individual such as a movie star or an organization with worldwide reach.

2. The media have publicized a fire that destroyed a family's home, leaving the parents and four children with absolutely nothing, not even a change of clothes for the children to wear to school "the day after". The community's response is often immediate, overwhelmingly generous, and heartwarming.

I want to make clear that I am *not* saying that you should not give to either of the above situations. I *am* saying that, before you donate, you should communicate with anyone responsible for handling the Tzedakah funds for these specific projects to find out "where they are at", i.e., how much money has already been raised and at what rate. You may also ask whether or not they have become aware of costs beyond what they had originally anticipated. With those facts in hand, you can then determine whether or not your own donation will be needed. The fact is, even though it is a classic "easy" money situation, there have been many times when the money just doesn't come in as expected. If this turns out to be the case, then you should definitely proceed with your plan to donate.

There is yet a third variation relating to the issue of "easy" money:

3. A well-connected organization has set a goal, say, of $10,000,000 for either a specific program or for its annual operating needs. The organization has a long history of raising the vast percentage of this enormous *absolute* sum from a small circle of foundations or individual millionaires. Your question should be, "If $275,000 can be raised from small contributions, could theyjust as easily raise all of it by making just one phone call?" If the answer is "Yes", you may want to use your Tzedakah money for other Tikkun Olam.

Here, too, there is an important exception. Sometimes the answer is "No". You may have found a Mitzvah program that has a large budget, but has low overhead, is efficient, and changes the lives of many people for the better. When you reach your trustworthy contact, if that person tells you that 22% of their budget comes from "small money" and that they cannot raise that money any other way — *then* you may decide that you want to donate, because your donation *will* make a difference.

One final note: While you are working with "easy" money situations, also consider the needs at the other end of the scale. Some Tikkun Olam programs are often unpopular, neglected or forgotten. One particular cause that is sometimes deemed unimportant is programming for individuals with mental illness. For various reasons, most of these endeavors struggle to raise sufficient Tzedakah money to change the lives of the people to whom they are directing their efforts. Quite simply: Raising $500,000 for a child's heart transplant is often easier than finding $10,000 for a socialization program for individuals recovering from mental illness.

Are There Principles, Practices, and Standards Used in the World of Business That Would Help You in Your Tzedakah Work?

Recently, many young, successful entrepreneurs have started to apply business principles and practices in their quest to help Tzedakah programs. In large part, this trend represents a positive contribution to Tikkun Olam. Using their talents, these enthused and idealistic people have helped many Mitzvah heroes and organizations streamline their operations, thereby making them more efficient and effective. They have emphasized strategic and long-range planning and the absolute need for fiscal responsibility. Their familiarity with the latest technology — hardware, software, graphics, and web design — has saved enormous amounts of previously-wasted money and brought in additional enormous sums for Tikkun Olam. Some of these "whiz kids" are simply dazzling.

You, yourself may want to consult with some of these Wunderkinder when you are planning your own Tzedakah strategy. If you do, it would be good to keep in mind that, while business principles and practices do often overlap, there are certain areas where you will need to differentiate between business and Tzedakah. American laws are different for both; the Internal Revenue Service has different regulations for both. You should also remember that Jewish principles may differ from secular laws and regulations.

The following is a list of several issues you may want to consider when you do your due diligence, i.e., your "homework":

Ethics: Are there different ethical rules that govern businesses and Tzedakah? Are there legal gray areas that in certain circumstances might be acceptable in business, but should be avoided in Tikkun Olam work? Should Mitzvah heroes and Tzedakah organizations be held to a higher standard? Is it appropriate to demand of a Tzedakah program that its work should not only involve no wrongdoing, but also *the appearance of* no wrongdoing?

Human relations: In either category — business or Tikkun Olam — is it permissible for a boss to be "tough", imperious, or condescending to employees they supervise? Is embarrassment or humiliation acceptable under any circumstance as a means of reaching a Tikkun Olam goal?

Human resources — hiring and firing: Is the method of hiring and firing the founder, the director, employees, and volunteers the same for both business and Tikkun Olam? Are people hired and fired according to Jewish principles? You have often heard of a new boss whose first order of business is to "clean house". In simple terms that means he or she fires staff members or officers and replaces them with others. Even if people were let go (in "housecleaning" or any other situation), is the process conducted in a Menschlich manner?

Formal training: Are formal degrees necessary either for business or Tzedakah work? Should a person with certain degrees *necessarily* have a higher position in the Tzedakah organization? These questions are separate from the issue of licensing. In both Tikkun Olam work and business, licenses, certifications and legal permits are absolute requirements.

Terminology: Are the business terms "CEO", "CFO", "CIO", and the like, applicable to people who direct non-profit organizations? When is it or isn't it appropriate? What is the message of applying business and professional terminology to Tzedakah work? Are there Jewish terms that could be used instead? What are the advantages and disadvantages of using the business or Jewish terms for each Tzedakah organization or Mitzvah hero that interests you?

Salaries: What is an appropriate salary for a non profit's executives and support staff? Is it sometimes, usually, or always true that these salaries be competitive with executives in the for-profit world in order to guarantee quality Tikkun Olam work? Does paying higher salaries *necessarily* mean that a smaller percentage of your Tzedakah money is reaching the intended recipients? Is an executive's dollars-and-cents track record of raising more funds for the organization sufficient justification for a high salary?

Boards of directors: Is the method of selecting board members the same for both? Is the relationship of the board of directors to the employees the same for both? Should the board members' relationship to the staff be different if they serve an all-volunteer Mitzvah organization? In the special case of a Tzedakah organization that is run by a Mitzvah hero, should the board's relationship be different?

Money management: In the business world, many formal and informal rules govern money management. For example, the Golden Rule of endowments—never touch the principal — would this rule apply to every Tikkun Olam situation? If not, under what circumstances would it be acceptable to suspend the rule? Is it permissible or appropriate for a Tzedakah organization to invest funds in a business, which is unfair to its workers, to the environment, or to society in general? Is it permissible for either business or Tikkun Olam groups to accept and use money whose source is, at best, questionable?

Risk: Are different kinds of risks permissible in Tikkun Olam that would not be considered sound business management? How would a "risk management specialist" evaluate "risk" for business and for Tikkun Olam?

Fungibility: In the context of Tzedakah organizations, "fungible" money means that it is interchangeable or moveable. Among several issues are (1) If you designate your donation towards one area of a Tzedakah program, can they then move already-budgeted money to some other aspect of the work? (2) If the organization *can* move money around in this manner, was this your intent when you donated the money?

Cost efficiency: May a Mitzvah hero or Tzedakah organization do things that are *not* cost efficient? If so, for what kinds of situations might this be acceptable?

The "Bottom Line": In business, the "bottom line" almost always refers to financial profits. What criteria would be appropriate for determining a non-profit's "bottom line"?

By comparing and contrasting these two worlds, I believe you will be able to make better decisions in your Tzedakah giving. Without question, these are serious issues. I believe that by evaluating and balancing, using your intelligence and your common sense, you will give more wisely. The end result will be even more and greater Tikkun Olam than you ever imagined.

How Useful Is the Internet
for Your Tzedakah Research?

There is no question that the internet can be a powerful tool if you want to give your Tzedakah money away judiciously and effectively. The power of search engines, and the world-wide reach that your computer affords you, anywhere, at any time, are awesome tools. Just consider that the United States alone has approximately 1,000,000 non-profit organizations. You can easily imagine just how valuable the internet can be as a first in your search for appropriate recipients of your Tzedakah dollars.

The Internet and Individual Tzedakah Programs

Today, almost any Tzedakah project of any size has its own website which will provide background information and a basic description of what it has set out to do, and, hopefully, what it is actually doing. What you will be looking for in addition to the basic information is (1) a real, i.e., snail mail, address — a post office box listing is not sufficient, (2) a list of the board of directors as well as the employees in charge of directing the use of the Tzedakah money, (3) a copy of the budget, and (4) a way to contact the project not only by e-mail but also by phone or letter.

Furthermore, if you are interested in contributing to an organization that allows you to donate online, you will want to know how secure that area of the website is. Most Tzedakah projects in the United States use a third party service such as **www.networkforgood.org** to process online donations. You will need to know what percentage of your donation will be used as a processing fee. Fortunately, many of them take a very low percentage, and, as this aspect of e-philanthropy develops, competition will inevitably keep the cost to a minimum. At present, many take 3% or less. You will need to decide if this is a wise and fair use of part of your Tzedakah money. Even more, you will need to decide whether you need to *add* to your donation to cover the fee. If your intention is to give $200, should you be giving $206, so that the recipient receives a total of $200? This is important "Tzedakah mathematics" you need to consider as you are giving your Tzedakah.

Of the highest priority: You will want to know if either the organization itself or the donation-processing service shares your personal information with other non-profits. You need to be assured that your e-mail address and other vital statistics remain inaccessible not only to other Tzedakah programs, but also to any unauthorized person *within* the organization to which you may be contributing.

The Internet and "Umbrella" Websites That Monitor and Evaluate Tzedakah Programs

Several websites will provide you large databases of non-profit organizations and people doing Tikkun Olam with Tzedakah money. Whatever research you do on the internet, remember that *this is only an initial step* in your quest to do meaningful and effective Tzedakah work. For all of the items below, and others you may discover, you must review the criteria on which they base their listings, analyses, and evaluations. For example:

1. Does the "umbrella" group only examine public documents?

2. Does it talk to or personally meet people who manage these organizations?

3. Has it spoken to people who work for these organizations, who work "on the front lines" where the actual Tikkun Olam is taking place?

4. How often are the data revised and reviewed?

5. Are there some organizations and Good People making a significant impact who are not listed because they are too small to be required by law to file a tax return with the IRS? (If a non-profit's activity is less than $25,000 annually, they are not required to file.)

6. Are there still others not listed because they are not even incorporated as a non-profit but are, nevertheless, doing exceptionally important Tikkun Olam work?

7. How can you find reports about family foundations which have to file a tax return, but are not required to provide a public record of their activities?

8. If one of these websites has a rating system, what is considered acceptable overhead for an organization to receive a good rating? (One such website allows 25% for fundraising and administration. In my opinion, this is much too high.)

9. And, finally, if one of these websites has a rating system of "the best", "acceptable", etc., what are the criteria for their choices? This is particularly important when you compare a Tzedakah program's ratings for more than one year. If, for example, one of them has risen or fallen in the ratings, you will need to know if you agree or disagree with how that change was determined. Sometimes the reasons do not correspond to Jewish values and/or your own personal sense of what is fair.

Following are some important websites listing American non-profits that may be of use to you.

1. **www.ziv.org** has more than 100 programs it is involved with in the United States, Israel, and other places in the world.

2. **www.guidestar.org** lists thousands of non-profit organizations, including their Form 990 which must be filed with the Internal Revenue Service.

3. **www.justgive.org** provides information similar to Guidestar's website.

4. **www.charitynavigator.org** examines the IRS 990 of 5,000 non-profits, and then analyzes and evaluates all of the data. It also compares and contrasts similar organizations, factoring in several important variables explained on its website. In addition, it lists each organization's donor privacy policy, its mission statement, and compensation for the organization's director.

5. **www.just-tzedakah.org** lists and analyzes hundreds of *Jewish* organizations and groups.

There are additional websites devoted to complete and thorough explanations of what to look for on a 990, Begin by looking at particular items and examine them carefully. The following is in no way definitive, but should serve as a guide and point of departure for your research:

1. What is the organization's total revenue?

2. What is the source/are the sources of the organization's revenue?

3. How much was spent on

   A. Program?

   B. Management?

   C. Fundraising ?

4. What are the organization's net assets?

5. How many people are on the organization's staff, and how much is their compensation?

6. The board:

   A. How many people sit on the organization's board?

   B. Who are they?

   C. Are they compensated in any way for serving on the board?

7. How much does the organization spend on travel and entertainment?

Again, these questions are merely a point of departure for your thorough investigation.

For Canadians, www.canadahelps.org lists every non-profit in the country.

For Israeli organizations, your starting point should be Professor Eliezer Jaffe's pioneering work, **www.givingwisely.org**. In addition to the issues raised above, it is of crucial importance to remember that laws and policies in Israel — and all other foreign countries — differ significantly from those in the United States. When you do your research on Israeli organizations, it is important to make contact with someone "on the ground" there, or someone here who knows the organization intimately, and, even more, how "the system" works over there. (Please note: Organizations with an "American Friends of" in their name, operate under *American* law.)

The more you examine both "umbrella" websites and their evaluation of non-profit organizations, and the websites of *specific* non-profit organizations, the more skilled you will become at interpreting what you read. If you are "not good at" finding, reading, and understanding how websites work, do not hesitate to ask someone who knows Tzedakah-and-the-internet to give you some guidance.

Ultimately, your analysis need come to include the full range of your critical abilities: Does what you read make logical and reasonable sense? Does the tone of the website make you feel comfortable, or is there something behind and beyond the words and images that is "not quite right"? Of great importance, too, is the question, "What is your overall 'gut feeling'?" It's like in computer language – WYSIWYG — what you see is what you get.

The end of the process: You will want to be in touch *directly* and *immediately* with the person you deem most appropriate within the Tzedakah organization. Then, *and only then*, proceed, deciding what part you want to play in this organization's Tikkun Olam work.

All this having been said, remember that you will discover that amazing numbers of Tzedakah programs are absolutely wonderful and are managed with the greatest integrity.

Should You Use Some of Your Tzedakah Money to Pay for Operating Expenses and Other Overhead Needs?

At certain times, yes.

For many worthy Tikkun Olam programs and Mitzvah heroes and their work, the greatest worry is finding the money to allow them to continue to function. For example, if they have recently established their program, anticipated and unanticipated start-up costs can be a serious impediment to the program's stability. In addition, sometimes the work they are doing has found a way to solve a problem more broadly, profoundly, and efficiently than any other existing structure. Even with the best planning, the demand for their Mitzvah work may have grown rapidly. Occasionally, it grows so quickly and so unexpectedly, there was no way anyone could have anticipated the demand. They become overwhelmed by requests from all quarters and need to expand just to keep pace with the demand for their services.

Even though most donors would prefer to actually pay for a scholarship "to send a kid to camp", or to buy food for people who are hungry, it is important to consider that Mitzvah heroes and Tikkun Olam programs could do their work much more effectively by upgrading their computers, or adding a staff member to assume administrative responsibilities that would free the World Changers to do what they do best. Mitzvah heroes need time to devote their energies to the lives of others, offering them opportunities, hope, and life-saving services. And, they need to do it in their own unique way. In situations such as these, it would be proper — even recommended — to use some of your Tzedakah money to pay for the printing of brochures, rent, insurance, tax preparation costs, or similar overhead items. Your Tzedakah "investment" will extend the reach of the Tikkun Olam program many times over in two ways: (1) The program will gain greater support and reach more people in need, and (2) as noted above, it will free those doing the Tikkun Olam work to do what they do best, i.e., front-line Repairing the World.

It is, of course, your own choice how you want to balance your contributions for overhead with direct, immediate Tikkun Olam. Whatever your final decision, it is important to keep in mind that, at certain times, and for certain Mitzvah heroes and projects, you should consider both to be legitimate uses of your Tzedakah money.

What Should You Do About Mail and Phone Solicitations?

From the explanations given elsewhere in this guide, it should be clear that, unless the mail solicitation includes satisfactory financial information, you have no obligation to give. In fact, Maimonides and subsequent Jewish legal rulings state that you should *not* be giving to that organization. With solicitations over the phone, your procedure should be similar and relatively simple: Ask the solicitor to mail or e-mail you the organization's financial reports. If the organization does not, then your obligation to give ends there. If it does, and you are satisfied with what you learn about their fiscal responsibility, *then* you can decide whether or not you want to contribute.

A true story: One rabbi was so overwhelmed with mail solicitations, he felt he needed to contact me. He sent me a *seven-page list* of all the organizations asking for money, and a check for Ziv Tzedakah Fund, the non-profit organization I founded. As a rabbi, he naturally had many other responsibilities, and while he had the time to do *some* research on his own, he simply did not have enough time to investigate responsibly. Since he knew that there were several on his list that I trusted, he asked me to distribute his Tzedakah money as I deemed appropriate.

What If a Tzedakah Organization (1) Has Slick Publicity, (2) Keeps Sending You Mail, or (3) Gives or Sells Your Name to Other Tzedakah Organizations Without Your Express Consent?

In each of the three cases noted above, you may feel reluctant to donate. I will address each separately, but as you read my comments and consider whether or not to continue to send money, remember that there may be groups other than these that are doing equally fine or better work in the specific "field" of Tikkun Olam that interests you:

1. **Slick publicity**: Included in this category is an organization that has a very sophisticated website, and/or a highly professional-quality video/DVD. In most cases, you will be hesitant to donate because you believe that it is spending far too much money on overhead. You are more than likely correct, but there is one exception — when someone who believes in the Tikkun Olam work of the group has created the publicity for free, at cost, or at a greatly reduced price. Check to see if such a notice appears anywhere on the publicity. If not, and, if you really believe in the organization's work, contact the person in charge and ask for the details. If he or she says that the work was done for free or at a significant discount, you may want to suggest that the group state that explicitly. If it was *not* done for free, at cost, or at a reasonably reduced price, politely convey your dissatisfaction, and suggest the group change its policy, as you would be reluctant to continue to donate if it is spending so much money on publicity and fundraising.

2. **Mail overload:** Mass mailing is a decades-old industry which has been studied and analyzed from every angle. While mass mailings serve an important function for many businesses, individuals, and Tzedakah organizations ("kosher" and otherwise), be aware that a 3% return rate is considered high for many types of these mailings. In and of itself, mass mailings handled by professional mailing houses are not "bad", though I am generally opposed to them in the Tzedakah world. Again, if this is an organization that meets so many other good criteria, you will want to (1) contact the person in charge and ask how much was spent on the mailing(s) compared to how much Tzedakah money was actually received, and (2) you may ask to be removed from the mailing list, since you feel that you are being "overwhelmed" by the mail, and it is giving you second thoughts about the good work the organization is doing. You may add that you feel that, as "effective" as mass mailing may be for raising funds, you believe it is ultimately counterproductive. It may cause others to stop giving not only to this organization's Mitzvah work, but also to Tzedakah in general.

3. **Giving or selling your name to other organizations without your express consent:** *In no uncertain terms, this is unethical Jewishly and a severe abuse of the donor.* At this point, it is not enough to tell the group that you want to be dropped from the mailing list. You will also want to inform them — preferably by phone, or if possible, face-to-face — that you believe this is a violation of Jewish ethics.

How Much of Your Tzedakah Money Should Be Directed to Tzedakah Programs in Israel?

When you are deciding how much of your total Tzedakah budget to devote to Israel, you will need to keep in mind that there are many *unique* issues to be considered. A very short list includes:

    1. The continued influx of immigrants coming from Ethiopia, the Former Soviet Union, Europe, America, and other parts of the world;

    2 The enormous toll terrorist attacks have taken, not only on the loss of human life, but also the cost of rehabilitation of tens of thousands of physically and psychologically injured survivors;

    3. The economic drain on Israel's economy due to the demands of a high defense budget,

    4. The fact that, other than some select non-Jewish groups, the greatest percentage of financial support must come from the Jewish community.

In addition, in recent years, American Jews have demonstrated less commitment to Israel and its needs. This is a trend that most certainly needs to be reversed.

In light of all of these factors and many others I did not list, giving to Israel ought to be a fundamental area of your Tzedakah giving.

With that understanding, you may find it helpful to consider two approaches to your Israel Tzedakah donations. The first is largely described above — Israel's *unique* needs. The second involves Tzedakah for individuals, groups, and Tikkun Olam programs that are common to people everywhere. One of these needs is most basic — hungry people and people who live with what is called "food insecurity". This recently-coined term refers to people who, even if they have today's and tomorrow's food, still live constantly in doubt about the meals for the next day and the day after that. Additional common social needs include: people who are living on the financial edge, kids who have an educational experience that could be 100% or 200% better if the resources were available, health care needs, etc. The list is very long. You, yourself, could easily name another dozen.

There is a relatively simple technique to help you consider this second category, i.e., "common" needs. While you are deciding how to use your Tzedakah money, make a habit of putting the word "Israel" before the general category. For example, you may be particularly concerned about people who have Alzheimer's. You could give to Alzheimer's programs in the United States, but by making the mental note, "Israel — Alzheimer's", you may also consider using Tzedakah money for effective programs in Israel that need your support. The same would be true, for example, for "at-risk children" – "Israel — at-risk children", "people with special needs" – "Israel — people with special needs", and "Elders living with dignity" "Israel — Elders living with dignity". **www.ziv.org** will be a useful website for exploring both types of needs in Israel — the unique and the common.

How you *ultimately* decide which percentage of your Tzedakah money goes to Israel's unique or common needs, is, of course, your personal decision. Nevertheless, I personally believe that giving significant percentages of your Tzedakah money to Israel should be a major component of every Jewish person's financial commitment.

What If Someone Is Hungry?

The classic Jewish text concerning this question is as follows:

ורב יהודה אמר: בודקין לכסות ואין בודקין למזונות

Rav Yehuda said,
We may investigate when someone asks for clothing;
but we do not investigate when the need is for food. Bava Batra 9a

Rav Yehuda's statement, incorporated in the codes of Jewish Law, is intended for individuals *literally* asking for food in your presence. In that kind of a situation, there is no way of knowing if a delay might cause severe complications or even death. A Talmudic story (Ta'anit 21a) about Nachum Ish Gamzu is generally referred to as proof. He was riding on a donkey leading a second donkey laden with food supplies. A man approached and said, "Rabbi, feed me." Nachum replied, "Wait until I unload [the food] from the donkey's saddlebags." By the time he had begun to get the food, the man had died. This is an extreme case, but the truth is that you can never know how close another person is to dying of starvation.

Again, this text applies to someone who is *directly* asking for food. The issue is the very thin line between a human being who is still alive and שעת יציאת הנשמה, the very moment of death, when it is too late to do anything. A conversation a doctor or nurse will help you focus on the extreme urgency of that unique moment.

Should You Give to People in The Street?

I am frequently asked this very difficult question.

The Jewish short answer is, "Yes".

The fact is that many questions arise when you do so. Among them are:

1. What if they just use it to buy alcohol or drugs?

2. As I walk to work, what if there are so many of them, I couldn't possibly provide for all of them?

3. If I keep giving to them, won't this strain my Tzedakah budget to the limit?

4. Wouldn't it be better to buy them a meal?

A more thorough Jewish response is beyond the reach of this guide. However, Arthur Kurzweil wrote an extensive, eminently-readable, and well-organized study several years ago. It is still the best treatment I know on this subject. [It also has one of the best titles of any Jewish article I have read: *I Can't Read Much Hebrew, I Can't Read Much Aramaic, I Never Went to Yeshiva, But I Study Talmud Every Chance I Get. Brother, Can You Spare a Dime: The Treatment of Beggars According to Jewish Tradition: A Case in Point.*] You can read Kurzweil's article on the Ziv Tzedakah Fund website **www.ziv.org**. I believe it is essential reading for anyone interested in the *Jewish* view of this issue.

Tzedakah
and the Meaning of "Self"

מענטשלעכקייט איז מער פון אלץ
Being a Mensch is the most important thing.

Yiddish proverb

Who Benefits More, the Giver or the Recipient?

תני בש' ר' יהושע
יותר ממה שבעל הבית עושה עם העני
העני עושה עם בעל הבית

It was taught in the name of Rabbi Yehoshua:
The poor person [standing at the door] does more for the householder than
the householder does for the poor person.

Leviticus Rabba (Margoliot Edition) 34:8

Because of the very nature of Tzedakah, there are those who say that the giver gets more out of the act of Tzedakah than the recipient. People who are engaged in Tikkun Olam clearly benefit in many ways. Just a few of the benefits: You feel good, you feel a sense of accomplishment, and you acquire a sense of greater meaning in your life. This last glorious feeling was expressed nearly 2,000 years ago when Ben Azzai taught that, "ששכר מצוה מצוה‏-The reward for a Mitzvah is the Mitzvah itself." (Pirkay Avot 4:2) In and of themselves, Mitzvahs have the power to take a person into higher realms of meaning. Tzedakah most assuredly is one of the Mitzvahs that has that power…even if you have used your money to do something as "un-sublime" as paying the salary of a nurse's aide who changes diapers on adults who are no longer capable of caring for themselves.

All that said, I would humbly take issue with the great Rabbi Yehoshua of ancient Israel. While it is true that the giver benefits from having done a Mitzvah and feels good about having done it, the food in a hungry person's body far supercedes those benefits. So, too, having a new roof over one's head after a hurricane has torn the old one apart. In fact, I believe this is a general rule of Tikkun Olam: No matter what the benefits to the giver, the recipient's benefit is *always* more immediate and much more "real".

Will Your Personality Change If You Do More Tzedakah?

רב אמ' לא נתנו מצוות אלא לצרוף בהן את הבריות

Rav said:
Mitzvahs were given in order to refine human beings.

Leviticus Rabba 13:3 (Margoliot Edition)

The Pocket

Will your personality change if you do more Tzedakah?

It might.

It has for many people.

The Talmud records an interesting passage that addresses human personality:

אמר רבי אילעאי: בשלשה דברים אדם ניכר
בכוסו ובכיסו ובכעסו.

Rabbi Ila'i said:
A person's personality may be sensed by three indicators —
The cup [how the person handles alcohol],
The pocket [how the person uses money],
Anger [what kinds of things anger the person].

Eruvin 65b

"The pocket" — Rabbi Ila'i teaches that one sure way to know a person is to observe how a person uses money both for personal needs and for Tzedakah.

Many things make you feel good about yourself. But there really is something special about the *specific* good feeling that you have when you demonstrate how much you care for others. There is something extraordinarily attractive about alleviating another's worries, pain, or despair. What words are there, really, to describe how you feel when *you* have taken people whose sadness has overwhelmed them and caused them to feel better for a moment, for a day, a week, or permanently?

One Mitzvah and Then Another and Another

Furthermore, Tzedakah has the power to drive you to do even more Tzedakah. It is, in many ways, addictive in a most positive sense. Almost 2,000 years ago, the brilliant Ben Azzai stated it beautifully and succinctly: שמצוה גוררת מצוה — One Mitzvah exerts a pull on another. (Pirkay Avot 4:2) A friend taught me the same principle in more realistic terms. She explained, "Doing

Tzedakah is like eating potato chips. Just as you can't eat only one chip, so, too, with acts of Tzedakah. Doing one Mitzvah gives you a craving for the next." Either way, in Real Life, when you pay for home care aides to take care of Elders so that they won't have to go into a nursing home, that very act of Tzedakah may give you a profound sensation of wanting to do more earthshaking miracles. When you use your money to make a fine Passover meal for a new immigrant, buy life-saving medicine for a widow living on a pittance in Moscow, endow a special needs Torah study program in a day school — it becomes difficult to even think you want to slow down or stop. Just consider what it means to pay for birthday parties for kids somewhere who never had one...boys and girls you will never meet because you want them to know that *somewhere, someone really* cares about them. (

At Your Own Pace

Because everyone by nature is different, the power of Tzedakah can influence and shape people at different rates and at different times in their lives. People respond in various ways, and you would do well not to make comparisons with how others may have changed. For some, Tzedakah's intense attraction is like simple addition: one Mitzvah-money-generated deed generates another. Others may move exponentially: Buying three pairs of shoes for people whose own shoes are tattered may lead them to 3^3 — 27 more pairs. There are no guarantees, but most likely you will find yourself somewhere within that range.

You may possibly be someone who feels that you have some rough edges that cause irritation, embarrassment, or dismay in others. (I certainly do.) This may make you uncomfortable, and you find yourself living with a poor self-image. Or, you may be troubled that you have acquired a reputation for being condescending or abrasive. Consider one example: arrogance. At first glance, the awesome *power* of Tzedakah and *humility* would appear to be a classic contradiction in terms. And yet, since the essence of Tzedakah is both the Life-force and the spiritual affirmation of Life, you might feel humbled by this human gift. In theological terms, you would express gratitude to the Giver of Life for being allowed to spend your days doing Tikkun Olam.

Many Ways to Acquire a Sterling Soul

In the world of personality refinement, there are, of course, abundant and diverse methods to repair an injured psyche. Engaging in more Tzedakah is one such method which you may wish to keep in mind. As it has benefited others, it may also work well for you. Possibly, it will even work wonders for your Self. If you *do* feel a certain disappointment about the way you have treated others (and yourself), doing more Tzedakah can serve as a constant reminder that you *are* capable of being a deeply caring, even noble, human being. You can assure yourself that *ultimately* this is the kind of person you are.

To repeat the question: *Will my personality change if I do more Tzedakah?* Not *necessarily* and certainly not *automatically*. But you have changed the odds, and you have changed them far better than you might have expected. Tzedakah does not operate by the same rules as mathematics. Still, even though no precise "ratio of Tzedakah to positive change in personality" exists, you may very well find yourself kinder, more understanding, patient, and gentle than you were before.

Will You Be a Tzaddik/Tzadeket If You Give Tzedakah?

"I am convinced that the sense of meaning grows not by spectacular acts but by quiet deeds day by day."

Rabbi Abraham Joshua Heschel, ז״ל

Yes…at least at that moment of giving.

Unfortunately, the term "צדיק-Tzaddik (m)/צדקת-Tzadeket (f)" is too often translated "righteous person". Actually, it frequently means "a good person", "a Mensch." Grammatically, "Tzedakah" and "Tzaddik/Tzadeket" are from the same Hebrew root – צ-ד-ק. The language itself shows that there is an intimate connection between the Tzedakah-act and the person-doing-Tzedakah at any given moment. Still, Tzedakah-deeds are only *momentary* events in your life, occurring more or less frequently as you establish your own pattern of giving.

One Jewish text elucidates the connection between yourself and what you have accomplished by your deed:

מאי צדיק...בעל צדקות

"What is a 'Tzaddik'? A Tzedakah-oriented person (בעל צדקות-Ba'al Tzedakot)."

Kallah Rabbati, Chapter 8

What Jewish tradition is teaching is that doing the Mitzvah of Tzedakah *may*, *should*, or *could* lead to more than simply a string of giving-moments. Doing Tzedakah can become a regular point of reference and general framework for your way of life. If Life's goal, or one of Life's goals, is to become a Tzaddik-צדיק, then certainly giving Tzedakah is one way to achieve that goal…in conjunction. Of course, with a pattern of גמילות חסדים-Gemillut Chassadim, personal acts of caring, lovingkindness.

Understandably, there is a proviso. This text does *not* mean that a Tzedakah-oriented person who has a mean streak, is overbearing, or mistreats people in other ways can continue to behave in this fashion. Being a lousy human being and a Ba'al Tzedakot-בעל צדקות are a contradiction in terms.

In one of his sermons, my teacher, student, and friend, Rabbi Mark Greenspan, explained this entire issue most eloquently:

Maybe we're a little uncomfortable with this idea, but Judaism teaches us that each of us has the potential to be a Tzaddik…No one has a right to say, 'I'm just an ordinary person trying to make a living.' Each moment has the potential for greatness. We must look for those special moments. Judaism challenges us to strive for righteousness in our lives,

not by doing great things, but by doing ordinary things, by living an
ordinary life that makes a difference. Winston Churchill once said:
"We make a living by what we get. We make a life by what we give."

Rabbi Greenspan is correct on both counts: that anyone can strive to be a Tzaddik, that it is a good and right thing to do, *and* that this very grand goal can be achieved…*"by doing ordinary things, by living an ordinary life that makes a difference."*

What Benefits Will You Receive, What Dividends Will Accrue, and What Return Will You Get on Your Investments When You Give Tzedakah?

There is a wonderful story from Talmudic literature that answers this question most eloquently beyond The Big Four, namely: (1) Financially, if you give to a tax-exempt organization, you get a tax deduction; (2) psychologically, you feel good; (3) spiritually, you have a sense of meaning in your life, and (4) physically, you are invigorated.

The story goes as follows:

In the 1st century of the Common Era, there was a Jewish kingdom in a place called Adiabene in what is presently modern-day Iraq. King Munbaz II, son of Queen Helena and Munbaz I, did a most curious thing — he emptied the royal treasury and used the money for the benefit of his subjects who were in need.

According to one version (Bava Batra 11a), a calamitous drought had devastated his kingdom. Another text (Jerusalem Talmud, Pe'ah 1: 1) doesn't record any specific stimulus, which would imply that King Munbaz had reached the stark realization that his subjects normally had enormous pressing needs. Whichever account you study, you can certainly understand that his relatives were not at all pleased with what he did. Here is their exchange with the king:

שלחו לו קרוביו ואמרו לו
אבותיך הוסיפו על שלהן ועל של אבותיהן
ואתה ביזבזתה את שלך ואת של אבותיך
א"ל כל שכן
אבותי גנזו בארץ ואני גנזתי בשמים...
אבותי גנזו אוצרות שאין עושין פירות
ואני גנזתי אוצרות שהן עושין פירות...
אבותי גנזו במקום שהיד שולטת בו
ואני גנזתי במקום שאין היד שולטת בו...
אבותי גנזו ממון ואני גנזתי נפשות...
אבותי גנזו לאחרים ואני גנזתי לעצמי...
אבותי גנזו בעולם הזה ואני גנזתי לעולם הבא...

His relatives sent him a message, saying, "The generation before you accumulated even greater treasures than their ancestors. Now see what you have done! You have wasted both your own wealth and that of your ancestors!"
King Munbaz replied, "I have outdone them all.
"My ancestors accumulated earthly things; I have gathered things for Heaven....

"My ancestors saved money that did not pay dividends; my money is paying dividends....

"My ancestors stored things that could be stolen; mine can't be stolen....

"My ancestors amassed money; I have collected souls....

"My ancestors hoarded things that wound up in the possession of other people; what I have done will always be mine....

"My ancestors held on to things for this world; what I have is being held in The Next World."

In a preceding chapter, I mention that Jewish tradition does not allow for giving away more than 20% of your income except in extreme and clearly-defined circumstances, one of them being that wealthy people may give away more. I suspect that the usual "maximum 20% rule" applies to us "regular people" and that somewhere, somehow, Munbaz had additional funds to provide for his own needs. However you choose to explain that aspect of the tale, Munbaz's answers are eloquent, beautiful, and profound. They express the true benefits and dividends of giving Tzedakah.

Is There a Connection Between Money and Wisdom?

אמר רבי ישמעאל
הרוצה שיחכים יעסוק בדיני ממונות
שאין לך מקצוע בתורה גדול מהן שהן כמעין הנובע
והרוצה שיעסוק בדיני ממונות ישמש את שמעון בן ננס

Rabbi Yishmael said:
Whoever wants to acquire wisdom should study the laws relating to
money matters (civil law), because there is no Torah-subject greater than
this. This topic is like an ever-flowing stream. And whoever studies the
laws of money matters should be an intern with Shimon Ben Nannas.

Bava Batra, last Mishnah

Rabbi Yishmael's teaching seems to mix two realms of human experience — (1) the high and abstract, i.e. wisdom, and (2) mundane situations based on very commonplace experiences. The following comments should help clarify Rabbi Yishmael's words:

Wisdom: Meaning — the power to take accumulated knowledge and experience and grasp certain rules, truths, and principles about the world, Life, and human beings. "Wisdom" means to move beyond the simplistic, such as "All people are basically good." "Wisdom" means that the terrorists who flew their planes into the World Trade Center and Pentagon were evil people. "Wisdom" means to incontrovertibly reject arguments such as, "Well, Hitler kept the trains running on time." *Jewish* wisdom tells us that we do not achieve wisdom by starting from an intellectual blank page and then building a theory. Rather, wisdom comes by studying significant Jewish texts, assimilating the relevant facts, analyzing experiences, and reflecting on human reactions and interactions in individual real-Life situations. Then, and only then, should you move on to more general principles.

Study the laws relating to money matters: If you want to take basic, earthy examples of human interaction, you won't find a better field of observation than civil and criminal cases involving money. Page after page of the Talmud deals with these issues, and, even though the arguments are often very complicated, you do not have to be an attorney to understand the topics under discussion. Just think for a moment about all the money issues you have encountered in the media: lawsuits both just and frivolous, fights over wills, fraudulent insurance claims, protesting the protesters not wanting a group home for adults with special needs in your neighborhood, fences, fines, alimony and child support issues, personal injury claims, negligence, unfair labor practices, deceptive business practices, returning merchandise, refunds, perjury, loans, scheduling debt repayments, assault and battery, and harassment, all barely touch the range of issues. And one way or another, you know about them.

Ever-flowing stream: The subject matter will nourish and continue to nourish your Jewish soul like water to a thirsty body.

Intern with Shimon ben Nannas: Everyone needs an expert to help him or her work through the complexities of the issues of interpersonal relations. It is more than just clerking with a circuit court judge. Interning with Shimon means not just *learning* the law and how it works, but also whether or not it is just, and, if not, how the law can be changed. Because he was not only a legal expert, but equally important, steeped in *Jewish* law and Judaism as a way of life, discussions of priorities would also include justice and mercy in the law, the law as derived from divine sources, rulings based on an awareness that not only human beings are following the flow of history, but also God, Creator of heaven and earth, who freed us from the Land of Egypt, and gave us this freedom to do Tikkun Olam. *Everyone* needs a guide such as Shimon ben Nannas.

That is the intimate relationship between money matters and wisdom.

In Conclusion —
Four Stories from "Real Life"

Diapers:
Where Tzedakah Begins and Sometimes Ends

On Ziv Tzedakah Fund's behalf, Naomi Eisenberger, Managing Director, recently began to explore an area of Tikkun Olam that Ziv thought it may have neglected — supporting both elderly Shoah survivors living in Israel and righteous non-Jewish rescuers who had arrived since 1945, and made Israel their home. All of them, of course, are Elders.

Ziv's way of making this happen has always been to find someone, some one, or two, or three individuals, whom it knows and trusts who can act as its agent and connect it to individuals in real need. Just yesterday, Ziv got its first report. This report was about Righteous Gentiles who had saved Jews. We were told the stories of four such individuals, one even responsible for having kept more than 25 Jews alive. Each story moved me deeply, and I found myself pausing between each because what they had done was so awesome, so *human* to the greatest degree I could imagine. The report's summary was two-fold: a short biography and a list of what each one needed the most. Some needed additional caretaker help for 10 hours/week @ X number of dollars/week. One needed some basic repairs on his apartment, the estimated cost being well within the range of Ziv's funds. And, two of them needed an ongoing supply of adult diapers.

Diapers. I kept thinking about the diapers. Even with Arnie Draiman, Ziv's representative in Israel, finding an excellent price, four or five diapers a day for two people for an initial period of four months, came to a lot of money. I kept thinking, "So it has come to this. Diapers for people who risked their lives to save Jews." At the same time I remembered how I squirmed in my chair the first time that I saw a television commercial about diapers for adults. It was another one of those unmentionable topics that had been exposed. Now the sanitized pictures that had appeared on my screen a few years back, took on a very different meaning. Murder squads. Gas chambers. Crematoria. And acts of courage in the midst of human cruelty the likes of which had never before been seen in human history.

The rescuers will get their home care assistance, the repairs, and the diapers. It's the least anyone could do.

Mitzvah Shopping

One of Wilshire Boulevard Temple's Darfur Relief Projects

In the spring of 2005, I was invited to spend six days at Wilshire Boulevard Temple in Los Angeles. It is a *very* large congregation, with more than 2,000 family units. I was invited both to lecture as well as to be a participant in several programs. Each session was a unique experience, and each was pleasant and satisfying in its own way. One program in particular stands out as something I had never experienced before in all of my 31 years of work in this field — Kids' Mitzvah Shopping Night at Costco.

The background: The congregation was about to ship a huge container of donated goods to the Darfur region of Sudan. The slaughter and suffering in Sudan has been going on for years, and, at this writing, still shows little sign of abating. The congregation had already done the most important piece of research. They had located an agency in Sudan that could assure the members that the donated goods would arrive safely and would be delivered directly to some of the thousands of Sudanese in refugees camps. Arrangements had also been made for the actual shipping of the container. All that remained was to fill it and to have it put on board the ship.

The synagogue arranged for its members to donate in one of two ways: (1) the congregation supplied cartons to any members who wanted, which the members could then fill with suggested items, or (2) they could donate money, and volunteers and staff members would purchase the items.

Enter "The Kids"

The shoppers were a recently-formed group of post-Bar and Bar Mitzvah students who would be focusing their efforts on Tikkun Olam. Months before, when Rabbi Dennis Eisner and I were reviewing my schedule, I told him I was particularly excited about this program. Even the name excited me: "Mitzvah Madness". I just *knew* that the educators would be teaching Tzedakah with great creativity.

The night the teen-agers went Mitzvah shopping, they had $2,100 of Wilshire Boulevard's Tzedakah money at their disposal.

This was the scene at Costco: Eight students, their educators, two or three assistants, and myself as a participant, came in for a special kind of shopping spree. A few minutes before, one of the educators talked to the manager about what we were planning to do; he kindly offered us a big lawn table and chairs in the middle of the store so we could sit together and talk as a group.

Money, Money — The Counting of the $100 Bills

Until this point, the kids did not know exactly *how much* money they had to spend. The educators explained the program, including a basic list of what kinds of items were needed, and what could and could not be shipped more than half way around the world to Sudan. Then one of the leaders took out twenty-one $100 bills and counted it out right in front of them. The kids' eyes lit up, and the buzz and chatter began. It felt like a younger version of a family's first reaction when it finds that out one of its members just won the lottery. Sometimes money does that to kids, just like it does when they are older and Big Money suddenly becomes part of their lives.

The truth is, though, I could tell that they already began to "get it". Deep in their gut they knew that this was not *their* money, not then, not in a half hour, never. It was Mitzvah money that would buy critically-needed items for utterly-despairing people living in a nightmare. Even before they put their hands on big shopping carts, I knew that not one of them imagined that a single penny of this was for themselves.

They proved it once they began pulling huge quantities of merchandise off of the shelves. And they proved it to themselves.

Up and Down the Aisles

Some more details: We broke up into three groups of two or three students and a staff member or two, in case there were questions. Let me make it clear, though — it was the teen-agers who ultimately made the choices, put their own hands on the merchandise, and put it in the carts. Now and again they might ask each other or a staff member whether product X or Y was appropriate since it hadn't been specifically listed among the recommended items. I was particularly struck when one of them looked at the brooms and suggested that they put a bunch of them in the cart. One of the group responded by describing what a refugee camp must be like — tents, no real floors, just dirt, and the like — and that brooms weren't necessary. It was a stunning moment. Kids, most of them so-called "privileged" children, kids talking High Tzedakah to each other, "getting" it.

Checking out

While one of the staff took care of check-out, the rest of us then had some time to discuss what we had just experienced. As we reviewed the activity, I remember thinking again, "*Never once* did they think that this money was for themselves. Not a nickel of it." I was also impressed that had these kids been shopping for themselves, they could have easily spent all of the money. Many, but not all, of them are from well-to-do families and quite possibly wouldn't even flinch at spending $500 or $1,000. It was clear, though, that they had really learned the difference between "*shopping* shopping" and "*Mitzvah* shopping". There is one thing, though, that they didn't "get". They had succeeded in spending only about $1,550. They were new at Mitzvah shopping on such a grand scale, and couldn't get used to the fact that they could have bought 20 of some items instead of a dozen, or 50 instead of 30. But that will come with time as they grow up, earn their own money, and begin to do Tzedakah with their own resources.

When it was all over that evening, we filled a huge van with the purchases. On Sunday, it would be loaded into the container which would be picked up later in the week. Then, it would be put on the ship to work its way, so far away, to the refugee camps. In fact, by Sunday, it was already evident that the temple would need a second container because the congregants had donated so much.

It was quite an evening, and a few days later, quite an afternoon working with congregants to load up carton after carton of Tzedakah items for people they would never meet but who were, in some very intimate way, part of their lives.

Down at the Triple-T Truck Stop

Years ago in one of my books, I re-told a story I had read in the newspaper. It was about a certain Ira Morris, who owned a truck stop in Arizona called the Triple-T. The story interested me for two reasons. First of all, I had once been a truck driver. For 10 months during 1972-1973 I drove The Atid-United Synagogue Bookmobile around the country. It was a 29′ vehicle filled with Jewish books that were sold at — as best as I recall — 134 stops I made along the way. So, I had been in a few truck stops in my day, even though compared to the humongous semis parked to the right and the left of the bookmobile, mine seemed a little bit like a toy. Still, miniature truck or not, I was a trucker and my Mom and Dad were proud that they had raised a kid who had gotten two bachelor's degrees in four-and-a-half years of college and then a master's in another couple of years...seven years post-high school in all. They felt good that all that 20th century comparative literature, Bible, and Talmud would serve me well riding high on the interstates.

The second reason had more to do with what made the Triple-T different than other truck stops. Mr. Morris had added two elements no one else had thought of — a rocking chair and a very friendly cat. Both were available to any trucker who might need a special break beyond a standard long-haul driver's meal and cup of coffee before heading down the road again. They could pick up the kitty, sit in the rocking chair, and relax for as long as they wanted. Clearly, everyone was happy: the trucker, the owner, and, without a doubt, the cat.

Now, years after reading that story, my mind is wandering and I am beginning to wonder —

Is it possible that a truck driver climbed into the cab less stressed out than he would have been without the break in the rocking chair with the cat on his lap? It's possible.

Did he drive just a few miles per hour slower, closer to the speed limit, and 20% more carefully because he felt good? Perhaps.

Did the driver stay 27% more awake because — aside the coffee — he was in a good mood? Maybe.

Because the driver was feeling good and that much more awake on the long haul, is it possible that this one driver avoided some obstacle in the road, prevented a jackknife, a pile-up, his dying in a twisted wreck, and the deaths of other drivers and passengers? It is entirely possible that all of that didn't happen.

When the driver got home, did he or she hug and kiss his or her spouse and children differently? Maybe.

Did *all of this* happen and not happen to this driver? There's really no way to know for certain, but it is possible.

To two drivers? Possibly.

To 10, 20, 50, 100 during the lifetime of a cat? Quite possibly.

How many more heartbeats were added to the world's total? Billions upon billions.

Grand total, how much did the rocking chair and 14 years of cat food cost?

You save one life, you save the world.

Joe the Butler

Years ago in another one of my books, I re-told a story I had read in the newspaper. It was about a certain Joe Lejman who used to dress up as a butler and serve in a local shelter for victims of domestic violence. I thought it was a brilliant idea. The article I had read was a short blurb, so there was only one incident-moment that the reporter chose to relate. I had hoped for more, but, in retrospect, and with years to reflect, I understand the reporter's wisdom. The incident was The Incident, the one that would teach us almost everything we needed to know about Joe Lejman and his marvelous Mitzvah.

As it happened, one day, Joe had finished serving a meal for the residents, then poured the coffee. He poured for one woman, and then lit her cigarette. She began to cry. She cried because she told Joe that this was the first time she could remember that anyone had done something nice for her.

Now, years after reading that story, my mind is wandering and I am beginning to wonder —

Is it possible that this woman regained every shred of her lost self-respect because of Joe Lejman's single act of unadulterated caring and radiant goodness? It's possible.

Did she then tell the social workers she had emerged from her despair, regained her energy, and wanted to go job hunting the next day? She might have.

Did she then get a job, give the appropriate portion of her first and every subsequent paycheck to Tzedakah, do homework with her kids at night, and help get them through high school and into college? Perhaps.

Did the children then go to college, graduate, get jobs, give the appropriate percentage of their first and every subsequent paycheck to Tzedakah, and raise their families to do the same? Maybe they did.

Were the other women in that shelter so inspired by what she did that they did the same, start life all over again because of Joe Lejman? Maybe they did, too.

How many more heartbeats were added to the world's total? Billions upon billions.

How far out into the entire population of Planet Earth did the concentric circles reach because Joe Lejman, one man, got this crazy idea to be a butler in a shelter for women, who, by all reasonable possibility, should have sunk into lifelong oblivion?

Grand total, how much did Joe spend on a butler's outfit?

You save one life, you save the world.

Glossary
of Hebrew and Yiddish Terms

Abba (H): father.

Bima (H): The synagogue platform where the rabbi and cantor stand to lead religious services.

Chuppah (H): the wedding canopy spread over the bride and groom during the marriage ceremony.

Eema (H): mother.

Halachah (H): Jewish law.

Havdalah (H): the ceremony at the end of the Sabbath and holidays that makes a separation between the holy days and the secular days.

Kavod (H): dignity, respect.

Kishkas (Y): guts, intestines.

Mensch (Y; adj.-Menschlich): abstract-Menschlichkeit): an upright, responsible, decent, caring, compassionate person.

Mezuzzah (H): a small container holding an inscription from the Torah that is hung on the doorposts of Jewish houses. According to Deuteronomy chapter 6, it is to serve as a reminder to both residents and guests of God's presence in the house.

Midrash (H): Jewish literature from the first 7 or 8 centuries of the Common Era containing stories, aphorisms, and narratives. Also, any non-legal portion of the Talmud. Also used to refer to a specific story or tale.

Minyan (H): Quorum of 10 people required for community prayer and certain ceremonies.

Mitzvah (H): literally "commandment" or "instruction" — good deeds done by people according to the prescriptions of traditional Jewish texts, such as visiting the sick, comforting mourners, and giving Tzedakah. In this book, Mitzvah is usually synonymous with Tzedakah.

Pushka (Y): a Tzedakah box.

Rabbanit (H; Y=Rebbetzin): a Rabbi's wife.

Shabbat (H, Y=Shabbas): the Sabbath. "Shabbat Shalom," a Shabbat greeting — "A peaceful Shabbat to you."

Shoah (H): the Holocaust.

Shulchan Aruch (H): Joseph Karo's 16th century code of Jewish Law, considered to be a basic text for Jewish legal decisions.

Siddur (H; pl.: Siddurim): a prayerbook.

Simcha (H, Y): joy, a joyous moment, a celebration.

Talmud (H): an immense compendium of discussions, tales, aphorisms, legal give-and-take, and insights about Judaism, developed in Jewish academies (Yeshivas) during the first five centuries of the Common Era.

Tchatchka (Y): a toy, a knick-knack.

Tikkun (H): fixing up, repairing. Tikkun Olam = repairing the world.

Torah (H): literally "teaching". Originally meaning the Five Books of Moses, expanded to include the entirety of Jewish study and learning. "to talk Torah" is to discuss these texts.

Tzedakah (H): the distinctly Jewish method of performing charitable acts. From the word "Tzedek," Justice.

Tzedek (H): Justice.

Yahrtzeit (Y): anniversary of someone's death.

Yeshiva (H): school for Torah study.

Yom HaAtzma'ut (H): Israel Independence Day.

Yom HaZikaron (H): The Day of Remembrance of Israeli soldiers who have lost their lives defending Israel.

Yom HaZikaron LaShoah VeLaGevura (H): Holocaust and Resistance Remembrance Day, the day before Yom HaAtzma'ut, Israel Independence Day.

Yom Yerushalayim (H): Jerusalem Day, marking the recapture of all of Jerusalem in the Six-Day War of 1967.

Ziv (H): radiance.